# Democratisation in the Middle East
## Dilemmas and Perspectives

# DEMOCRATISATION IN THE MIDDLE EAST

*Dilemmas and Perspectives*

EDITED BY BIRGITTE RAHBEK

AARHUS UNIVERSITY PRESS

DEMOCRATISATION IN THE MIDDLE EAST
*Dilemmas and Perspectives*

Copyright © The authors and Aarhus University Press 2005
Edited by Birgitte Rahbek
Graphic design and cover by Jørgen Sparre
Printed in Denmark at the Narayana Press, Gylling
ISBN 87 7934 230 2

Aarhus University Press

Langelandsgade 177
DK-8200 Aarhus N
Fax (+45) 89 42 53 80
www.unipress.dk

73 Line Walk
Headington, Oxford OX3 7AD
Fax (+44) 1865 750 079

Box 511
Oakville, CT 06779
Fax (+1) 860 945 9468

Published with financial support from
The Plum Foundation

# Table of Contents

# Introduction
*Dilemmas of democratisation in the Middle East*

BIRGITTE RAHBEK

Democracy has been on the agenda in the Arab world for several decades, most particularly in the 1960s and 1970s when it was propagated by progressive and secular national opposition movements and parties – only to find no support in the West which, during the cold war, could only conceive of one enemy, the Communists or Socialists. Instead, the West supported and armed one authoritarian and repressive regime after another, shipping weapons of mass destruction and logistics to dictators. Socialists and pan-Arabists were seen as threatening elements, while the rising fundamentalists were considered a harmless counterweight. In the case of Afghanistan, however, the fundamentalists or Islamists were militarised and globalised by the West and set against the invading Soviet troops who were finally defeated and withdrew, leaving behind them tens of thousands of unemployed Mujahedeen eager for new exploits. A snake had been fostered at the imperial breast.

When the Islamists turned against their former sponsors and masters, democracy suddenly became the buzzword in the Western corridors of power, from whence it aimed more at foes than at friends in the Middle East. However, the creation of a Western style democracy, i.e. one man – and woman! – one vote in the Middle East, might lead to political structures different from the malleable and compliant ones favoured by the West. The long decades of despotism, corruption, and nepotism made it very likely that such a democracy would produce what the West now despised and feared most of all, an Islamist anti-Western nationalist regime.

Nevertheless the majority of Arabs (61 percent according to World

Values Survey in five Arab countries, Algeria, Jordan, Saudi Arabia, Egypt and Morocco) favour democracy over other political systems, which is a higher percentage than that found in 16 European countries and by far exceeds the figures in the US, Canada, Australia, and New Zealand. Yet it is the West that wants to export democracy to the Arab world in general and to the Middle East in particular, be it the American "Broader Middle East and North Africa Initiative" or the Danish "Wider Middle East Initiative". Both initiatives were inspired by the attacks on New York and Washington on September 11, 2001 but are not designed in such a way as to fulfil the democratic aspirations of the Arab peoples.

One of the mistakes of the West has been a tendency to consider the Arab world a static entity that should be pushed – by military or economic means – towards democracy. And one of the mistakes of the Arab world has been to blame everything on others, be it the US, the West in general, or Israel in particular. The essays in this book transcend both of these erroneous views and deal instead with both the external and the internal forces that are impeding or promoting democracy in the Arab world.

The new Western mantra demanding democracy has often been met with multiple accusations of double standards: "Why in Iraq and not in Saudi Arabia?"; "Why should Syria comply with the UN resolutions and not Israel?" and "Why is the latter allowed to have weapons of mass destruction and not the Arab countries?" Often raised yet never answered, these questions are on every Arab citizen's mind, and no plan for democracy and no amount of money can do away with them; at the end of the day they will have to be answered adequately and justly. Therefore it is out of the question to put the issue of the occupation of Iraq and Palestine aside and go ahead with business as usual with other Arab countries – as was the initial plan of, for example, the Danish government. No matter how forthcoming their leaders are, the people still demand justice and, surprisingly to some, no matter how dictatorial the leaders might be, their people still hold them accountable to some degree at least. Even a dictator has to listen to the street.

Furthermore the Arab world is, in its own fragmented way, still an entity. Men and women in the streets of Rabat or Damascus do feel an affiliation and empathy with the men and women in the ruins of Falluja or Jenin. The daily injustices imposed upon these people by their own rulers are repeated in the evening on TV, which shows pictures of occupation soldiers kicking in doors in Mosul or Ramallah.

Yet although the countries of the Middle East are changing, politically driven by internal forces, these current reform processes face a number of challenges. Internally, political opposition parties and factions, dissidents and NGOs are subject to varying degrees of control and containment by regimes whose popular legitimacy remains limited. While some of the regimes have started a dialogue with reform-oriented organisations and political factions, it remains to be seen whether this will generally result in comprehensive and enduring reforms and popular participation.

Furthermore, external actors – particularly the United States and to some degree Europe – are seeking influence on the political landscape of the Middle East, based on the notion that promoting democracy is the key to stability and prosperity in the region. However, these efforts are mistrusted by large sections of the Arab public, particularly in the wake of the US-led invasion of Iraq. Therefore the question is whether the approach represented by the West is appropriate and, if not, what alternatives are available.

In early February 2005 The Plum Foundation arranged a conference in Copenhagen in order to present "a view from the Middle East" on the dilemmas of democratisation in the area. The conference brought together a number of independent experts from Iraq, Saudi Arabia, Syria and Palestine, as well as a few Western scholars who for decades have been doing research, not only in and about the Arab world, but also among Muslims in Europe. The authors all focus on the challenges and possibilities arising from the latest developments in the region and the world at large. This anthology reflects the ideas and analyses presented at the conference and the chapters provide a broad and nuanced picture of the dilemmas of democratisation in the Middle East.

The main aim of the book is to provide a forum for opinions held by Arabs who are neither Western puppets nor fanatical nationalists or Islamists, but rather academics with a vast knowledge of the Middle East as well as of the West. The authors all support the building of a democratic secular Middle East, but their writings also show that although there is no easy way to achieve this goal, there are likewise no easy excuses for not making the attempt.

The book could be seen as complementary to the latest *Arab Human Development Report* and, as such, a much needed antidote to the sea of unfounded optimism as to the democratic outcome of the war in Iraq, as well as to the outcome of the various Middle Eastern "peace" initiatives.

In the first chapter *Nader Fergany* – the lead author of the *Arab Human Development Reports* – deals with the findings of these reports. Present Arab regimes have failed to deliver the goods to which the Arab people aspire both in terms of freedom – in the broadest sense of the word – and good governance, as well as concerning the minimum definition of development, namely economic growth. Nader Fergany outlines the future scenarios that are open to the Arab world, 1) a continuation of the status quo, i.e. "the impending disaster scenario"; recent developments in Egypt seem to confirm this viewpoint. 2) "The *épanouissement* scenario" with a redistribution of power, building of good governance, total respect of the key freedoms of opinion, expression and assembly, which again would lead to a higher level of civil participation. 3) Realistically speaking, however, this third scenario might lie somewhere between these two extremes. In Fergany's view there is no contradiction between Islam and freedom, and outside military interference, as in the case of Iraq, is counterproductive because one cannot liberate a people by depriving them of national liberation.

In chapter 2 *Raymond Hinnebusch*, professor of International Relations and Middle East Politics at the University of St. Andrews, discusses the structural conditions for democratisation in the Middle East. A secure national identity is often considered a prerequisite for democratisation, but the Arab states have struggled with borders being arbitrarily imposed on them rather than being congruent with local identity. Therefore loyalty to tribe and sect as well as to supra-state identities (Arabism, Islam) has competed powerfully with loyalty to the state, and overcoming this disunity – rather than establishing democracy – has been given priority by the leaders of these weak states. The same is true of the main popular political movements – pan-Arabists and political

Islamists – that have also been preoccupied with identity, unity and authenticity rather than democratisation. Where these movements have seized state power, state-building has often taken an authoritarian form. Hinnebusch argues that the international context is of utmost importance and – because of the pro-American policy of several Arab states – this has mainly been an impediment to democratisation, because it deprives the rulers of the national legitimacy which would allow them to risk democratisation.

In chapter 3 *Yezid Sayigh* draws on his experience as a consultant to the international donor community in Palestine in discussing how to translate talk about abstract or universalised concepts – such as accountability and democracy – into concrete policy and operational recommendations that are relevant to specific contexts with all their attendant political, legal-administrative, and constitutional legacies and social, economic, and cultural characteristics. Sayigh emphasises that the real concern is whether the fundamental changes can be achieved peacefully and "without imposing agendas and objectives that directly threaten the core values, ideals, and autonomy of other peoples". The chapter pinpoints the tendency of the West to extol outward or superficial aspects of a democratic process, e.g. elections, whereas the real problem lies in the proximity between those holding economic power and those holding military and political power, as well as the problem of the powerlessness of parliaments. Nor has economic aid to a country like Egypt, for instance, produced any democratic improvement; and, moreover, the heavily-promoted economic liberalisation policies tend to undermine democratisation. The role of the West concerning democracy in the Middle East can only be one of doing "least harm" whereas the crucial role can be played only by local democracy advocates and reformers.

In chapter 4 the Syrian scholar and dissident, *Samir Aita*, starts his essay with a brief overview of Syrian history since independence, under the simple but arresting headline "In the very beginning, there was democracy". The year 1963 delivered the *coup de grace* to an unstable democratic period and the present state of emergency in Syria was initiated in March of that year with the establishment of Baath rule. From 1970 until 2000 the Syrian power system was in the hands of President Hafez Asad.

After Asad's death in 2000 there ensued what Nader Fergany calls a "republican dynasty" marked by the ascent to power of Asad's son, Bashar. In his inaugural speech the young president mentioned the word democracy 16 times and thus gave hope to the Syrian intellectuals who launched the "Damascus Spring" in September 2000 with petitions and "salons" debating every aspect of Syrian social, economic and political life. A year later the regime cracked down on the most notable activists and put an end to the spring, although less brutally than in the past.

According to Aita, there are several components that constitute the basis of a sustainable democratic development: political parties; the relations between the State and the power system; the positioning of the business community; and, dealing with Islam – in particular radical Islam. The author guides the reader through the very intricate Syrian power web that guarantees weak state institutions and concentrates control and strength in the closed circles around the president. One of the key mistakes committed by the West is its inability to distinguish between the state and the power system. The same mistake was committed in Iraq when the US dismantled the state institutions.

British journalist *Graham Usher* who, for more than a decade, has covered developments in the Middle East from his base in Jerusalem analyses the current Palestinian struggle for democracy in chapter 5. This struggle, says Usher, takes place within "two contending, though still essentially modern notions of democracy: democracy as a vehicle of imposed reform and neo-colonial containment versus democracy as an instrument for popular empowerment and national liberation". The author lists various causes for the present crisis, namely the collapse of the Oslo peace process, the defeat of the second intifada, and Israel's unilateralism, i.e. the separation barrier and the disengagement plan. The Palestinian crisis itself has several components which include the concurrent crises of strategy, leadership, governance and legitimacy.

The Palestinian struggle for genuine democratic reforms has gone unsupported by either USA or Israel, because they both primarily regard "reform" to mean regime change. Thus, "The Americans, through Bush's 'vision' and the roadmap, hijacked the domestic Palestinian demand for democratic change and turned it into a means for containing the conflict and removing an elected, historical but insufficiently pliant leader".

Recent Palestinian elections have tilted the issue of democracy away from the US/Israeli conception of democracy as regime-change and conflict containment and back in favour of the Palestinians who view it as a means "not simply to improve governance, but fundamentally to build a society necessary for strengthening the Palestinian capacity to resist".

In chapter 6 *Hanan Rabbani*, Palestinian consultant for Amnesty International, deals with development aid as a new form of colonialism because of the increasing tendency to attach political strings to any kind of aid given, most particularly by the US. Rabbani writes: "Funding by the USAID programme has increasingly become conditional: Support for any Palestinian non-governmental organisation involves checking the history of every person on the board of trustees of the concerned organisation. This investigation is done in search of any political or social links or connections to anybody involved with Hamas". Recipient Palestinian NGOs are also required to sign a document denouncing "terrorism". Another side effect of this type of development aid has been that "many Arab NGOs started implementing meaningless projects for the sake of acquiring the funds, and these projects did not leave a long-lasting positive impact on the lives of women and other marginalised sectors in the society". Much time and money has been wasted not only in satisfying the donors' conditions for aid but also because of the donors' lack of understanding of Palestinian culture and conditions. Hanan Rabbani illustrates these claims with several cases. The author believes that as long as Arab NGO's remain financially dependent on European and other Western funding it is unrealistic to expect equal partnership based on mutual respect, exchange of experiences and cooperation.

However, Hanan Rabbani does not confine herself to simply criticising the West, but also acknowledges the marginalisation of Arab women due to the inability of the patriarchal Arab regimes to advance the position of women. She advocates in the end of her essay the importance of strengthening the Arab women's movement.

In chapter 7 *Mai Yamani*, (Saudi Arabia), research fellow with the Middle East Programme at the Royal Institute of International Affairs, Chatham House, argues that democracy means different things for the ordinary people in the area and for the US. For the Saudi rulers the question is "how to play the *game* of democracy". But the Saudi population – in an age of globalisation – knows that the rulers are "inefficient, corrupt and unable to offer leadership".

The Saudi rulers attempt to comply with external and internal demands for democracy by *partial* elections, where women and other groups are excluded. There was a general low voter registration and turnout, but this could be used to support the Saudi regime's claim that "the population is satisfied with the status quo". The elections do not mean a redistribution of power, but the regime is under mounting pressure from its own people and from the surrounding countries which have at least chosen a token democracy. "The more that there is talk about democracy with no tangible results, the more the anger and frustration. This anger is often expressed against America but it is really against the regimes themselves".

The Saudi people have lived for decades under the old "unspoken agreement: the state paid for everything and told them nothing. No taxation, no information". This situation prevented the development of any notion of accountability or transparency. By outlawing all kinds of civil liberties in Saudi Arabia "the ruling elite did not eliminate pluralism nor dissent but instead sent it underground and onto the worldwide web. Hundreds of these web sites exist; the most extreme preaching the ideas of al-Qaida and its ideological brothers".

According to Mai Yamani the ruling family has to establish a leadership and enter into dialogue with the people "with the explicit purpose of finding a new story of Saudi Arabia that has to be modern and aware of global trends. The story has to be inclusive of people that now feel so estranged".

In chapter 8 the Saudi sociologist *Fowziyah Abu-Khalid* opens her essay by stressing that, "the Palestinian issue is a key question for reaching an objective understanding of the region. It represents a personal as well as a national importance for most Arabs in order to be engaged in a productive dialogue with the West. Without realising and acknowledging the real meaning of a continuous and unjust situation of the Palestinian people it will be a mere illusion to see a constructive relationship between the West and the Arab world".

The author questions the intentions of the Western plans for democracy in the Middle East: "Are they based on understanding and recognition of the cultural values of the targeted society or are they based on superiority complex of one version of history which is the Western history?" From there Fowziyah Abu-Khalid proceeds to specify the internal dilemmas of Saudi Arabia today, i.e. the political structure of the country, the absence of freedom of speech, the denial of multiplicity, the invisibility of women and the absence of a codified legal system.

The chapter ends by quoting the petition presented in 2003 by a number of Saudi activists and academics to the then Crown Prince Abdullah, listing a number of suggestions and recommendations for political reforms in Saudi Arabia.

In chapter 9 *Amal Shlash* from Iraq presents the factors behind the democratisation deficiency in Iraq and provides some broad suggestions on how to overcome existing challenges.

Iraq is today one of the poorest countries in the region in spite of the fact that, because of its natural resources, it used to be one of the richest and most industrialised countries in the Middle East. The oil sector totally dominates Iraq's economy constituting 74 percent of its GDP, and the country depends entirely on oil export for financing investment and consumption expenditures.

Another main challenge is the necessity of changing the role of the state in Iraq, making way for a pluralisation of the political system and a transition from a centralised planned economy towards market economy. In the past the distinctive characteristic of the Iraqi economy was the excessive role of the state and the weakness of the private sector.

In order to find a way through these challenges the author suggests that firstly, major attention should be given on all levels inside and outside Iraq to the building of human capital through education, including technical and scientific education, and through the encouragement of a spirit of enquiry inside the educational institutions. Secondly, the income disparities should be reduced through a process of development geared to job creation. This requires the serious building of a new private sector in Iraq, including encouraging the establishment of private organisations. Thirdly, closing the gender gap will be necessary in trying to solve the development problems and to increase political participation. Fourthly, after being isolated for the last 25 years, the Iraqi economy needs to be reintegrated into the global economy. Amal Shlash concludes by stating that if democracy is to take root in Iraq, it must be built primarily by Iraqis in response to specific Iraqi conditions and needs.

In chapter 10 *Huda Al-Nu'aimi* states that the decision of the occupying power to dismantle the Iraqi state contributed to the spreading of chaos and has deprived the country of security and stability. Another fatal result is the explosion of cultural, ethnic, and sectarian divisions in the country, which formerly was one of the most secular societies in the Middle East but is now witnessing an upsurge in political Islam within both the Sunni- and Shi'a communities. This development constitutes a dangerous outcome for democracy in Iraq.

Another key question is what kind of system the future Iraqi state should have, whether Iraq should adopt a presidential or parliamentary system, and where should the decision-making power lie? The author ends by listing specific demands that should be met in order to secure the future rights of Iraqi women.

The main emphasis of this chapter is on the role of women in all spheres of Iraqi life, and Huda al-Nu'aimi specifies the political, civil, economic, educational and social rights of women in the future Iraqi society.

Several of the authors have stressed European responsibility for democratisation in the Middle East. And this issue is never more acute than in the discussion of Islamophobia in Europe, the subject in chapter 11, by Professor *Jørgen S. Nielsen*, newly-appointed director of the Danish Institute in Damascus. The author distinguishes between the East-European indigenous Muslims and the immigrants in Western Europe coming out of a very different historical background, namely immigrations into Europe along the routes of the old imperial relations between Europe and its colonies.

The younger immigrant generations have claimed their place in the public space but, as the 1990s went on, the discourse of fear of refugees and asylum seekers was increasingly overlaid with a discourse about Muslims. After the collapse of the Soviet empire, Muslims increasingly came to play the role as the "enemy" or the "other". Particularly after 9/11 it became clear that "where politicians in the past could sell themselves with visions they now sell themselves with responses to fear, i.e. protecting people against the imaginary dangers outside".

Among Muslims in Europe there has also been a growing apprehension concerning the intentions of the West. Jørgen S. Nielsen points to the irony that "Huntington is now nowhere more popular and more acknowledged than in parts of Arab and Muslim society. There is almost a mirror image between Huntington's "clash of civilisations" idea and political Islamism".

The question of the loyalty of Muslim and other minority communities within Europe is a question of give and take and of their being included in all aspects of social life. According to Jørgen S. Nielsen, "one of the most important things that European countries and societies can do is to leave as much breathing space as possible for Muslims and other immigrant groups, whether they define themselves as Muslims or something else is in this sense beside the point. They should be given space to work out for themselves how to integrate functionally within their new society. The vast majority want to integrate, and in my experience find very constructive ways of doing so without assimilating".

It goes without saying that the multifaceted historical, social and cultural map of the Middle East cannot be contained in eleven chapters; neither can its seemingly insurmountable problems. Yet the knowledge and experience contained in this book paves the way for a far more fertile and respectful platform for a future cooperation between political actors in the Middle East, the EU and the US. After reading this book there are no more excuses for continuing along the path of futile piecemeal plans and projects because it will no longer be possible to say that "we didn't know".

# The UNDP's Arab Human Development Reports and their readings

NADER FERGANY

*Gamal Ad-Din al-Afghani[1]: The seeds of reform*
*"...The structure of absolute governance is tottering to ruin,*
*so fight to the utmost of your strength to destroy its foundations,*
*not to remove and get rid of isolated fragments of it".*

This essay will be structured around four points. 1) A brief introduction to the Arab Human Development Report. 2) A brief analysis of what I call the predicament or the crisis in governance in Arab countries. 3) A presentation of an ideal society of freedom and good governance and 4) a discussion of alternative futures of freedom and governance in the Arab world.

## The Arab Human Development Reports

I deliberately do not call it the UNDP-Report but the Arab Human Development Report, because the defining feature of the report has always been that it is produced by an independent team of Arab scholars and intellectuals; it is not a standard UN report, that is actually why it has become so distinguished from other UNDP reports. The Arab Human Development Report started in the year 2001 as an attempt by "Arab intelligentsia" to engage the Arab nation in an intellectual debate on the prospects of human development as the report defines it; it has become a debate that is loaded with passion.

---

1   An Arab freedom fighter although of non-Arab origins.

Perhaps the most important finding of the first Arab Human Development Report which came out in 2002 is the now famous three deficits. The report identified three major problems that were considered to impede human development in the Arab world. These are deficits in knowledge, in freedom and in the empowerment of women. After the first report became a big success, the idea developed to produce three follow-ups to the first report, each one taking one of these deficits and doing an in-depth analysis of each deficit and presenting a strategic vision to overcome them in the Arab countries. Hence we ended up with a second report that appeared in 2003 on the knowledge deficit and ended up with a vision of building a knowledge society in Arab countries. Last year's report, which was delayed, came out in the spring of 2005 and is devoted to the very crucial deficit in freedom and good governance in the Arab countries. There has been some controversy surrounding the advent of the report by some governments. The US Administration and some Arab governments, especially Egypt, tried to suppress or modify the contents of the report. It seems that at least two governments, the American and the Egyptian, got a leaked copy of an earlier draft and were very displeased with it. The controversy has luckily been resolved with the UNDP taking the brave stand of agreeing to issue the report under their logo.

### Governance crisis and development

The crisis in governance or the predicament of governance in Arab countries can be summarised as follows, present Arab governments and regimes have failed to meet the aspirations of the Arab people. At the same time these regimes do not promise radical reforms from within. The essential conclusion is that if there is failure coupled with stagnation there is a need for change – but *radical* change, as I will try to explain.

The Arab regimes have failed to deliver on two levels at least. The first level is freedom and human development: our definition of freedom in the report coincides to a great extent with human development.

First, the minimum definition of development is economic growth. Although there is an illusion that some Arab countries are extremely rich, the Arab regimes have failed to deliver economic growth. In the Arab Human Development Report we documented the fact that in the last quarter of the twentieth century the rate of growth in per capita income, which is the standard measure of economic development according to international financial institutions, was the lowest among all regions in the world. Actually we put it in a rather dramatic way in the first report: that if the rates of economic growth that prevailed in Arab countries in the last quarter of the twentieth century prevails, it will take the average Arab citizen one hundred and forty years to double his or her income. So by that criterion Arab regimes have failed in spite of the illusion that at least some of our countries are very rich.

In fact we also documented in the report that the Arab region as a whole is not very rich. The standard characterisation has been that if you pool all the gross national products of all Arab countries it will not come to the GDP of Spain or Holland. So on purely economic grounds Arab regimes have patently failed.

Second, if we move to the much higher level of human development in which we worry about things like knowledge and freedom as measures of human welfare, the failure of Arab regimes is much more conspicuous. The second report documents the very severe deficit in knowledge acquisition in Arab countries, and the third report documents the very drastic deficit in freedom and in good governance in Arab countries. It is extremely important to note that our definition of freedom accommodates an important element relating to national liberation. So our definition of freedom is not restricted to individual liberties, but also calls for important elements of societal and national liberation.

## National liberation and foreign occupation

In the Arab world we have seen under the present governance regimes that national liberation suffers great losses. Take first the issue of direct foreign occupation; we started the century with one of the nastiest racist expansionist occupations, the one of Palestine. We have had it for fifty years. In the third millennium we will add to it the occupation of Iraq by a coalition led by the US and UK. The question of outside interference is extremely important. I do not think that heavy-handed interference like the one we have seen in Iraq for example is at all useful. To the contrary, it is totally counterproductive and this in spite of the elections that took place in Iraq in January 2005. Imagine yourself holding elections with 200,000 foreign forces stationed on your soil, and you are going to the polls to choose between lists where you do not know the candidates and their platform and you have not debated the issues. In addition you have at the time of the elections a government of American spies running the elections. In addition you have every voter threatened with losing his food ration or ID card if he or she does not go to vote; and with the ultimate consequence that a significant segment of the population decides to boycott the elections. What would be your judgement of that election? You would have had elections but you would have no democracy, you would have no good governance and eventually you would end up with a government that is based on fractional and denominational representation, which is contradictory to our essential requirements of good governance being based on citizenship for all. In my opinion it is a farce.

Today about ten percent of Arabs live under direct foreign occupation. If we add to this the lack of national self determination that would be associated with the presence of large foreign troops located in Arab countries, we can see that the percentage of the Arab population that has suffered a loss of national liberation and self determination is much larger than the ten percent. In fact we should add that present Arab government regimes have invited foreign troops to come back to Arab territories after decades of independence.

The second element of the predicament of governance, as I see it, is that in addition to this failure we have stagnation in terms of governance reform, and governing regimes in Arab countries are not promising significant reforms from within. Actually we are seeing major signs of deterioration; suffice it to mention the fact that some ostensibly republican regimes are being transformed to dynasties, born out of coincidence.

## Freedom and good governance

The Arab Human Development Reports are concerned with freedom on an individual level, as well as on the societal and national levels. But at the same time even on the individual level we are not restricting ourselves to civil and political liberties. We add to this freedom from all forms of curtailment of human indignity, i.e. you cannot be free if you are hungry, if you are sick, if you are poor, and so on. So we have a conception of freedom that is rather comprehensive and is actually synonymous to human development as the report defines it. Translated in terms of the human rights system, our definition of freedom accommodates all realms of human rights. It does include respect for civil and political liberties, as well as social, economic, cultural and environmental rights.

The report establishes a very strong link between freedom and a good governance regime, because freedom cannot be totally respected – especially in our comprehensive sense – unless we have a good governance regime. More importantly, freedom cannot be *preserved* without good governance and that is why our first requirement of defining a good governance regime is that it must safeguard, protect and promote freedom in the sense that we define it.

A good governance regime is based on effective popular participation and it is based on institutions. These institutions are required to operate efficiently with transparency and be totally accountable to the people. More importantly, all this has to be under the strict rule of law that is protective of freedom and applies to all equally. This law has to be supervised and implemented by strictly independent judiciaries, something which is lacking in many Arab countries.

This system of good governance not only protects freedom as we define it, but it also secures the right of citizenship to all and insures alternation of political power. Behind this definition lies an understanding of the essence of governance that revolves around two major axes. The first axis is the distribution of power: who owns power in society? And power does not only mean political authority, it is important to recognise political authority as well as wealth or economic power as two sides of power. In Arab countries we increasingly see a co-habitation of political authority and wealth, providing very clear inroads to corruption. So, at present power is concentrated in the hands of a few, a clique, who normally control both political authority and wealth.

The second major dimension of governance is the method of the *exercise* of power. At present power is exercised through authoritarian dominant individuals and not through institutions as we require in good governance. Hence, if we desire a good governance regime, we have to do something about these two axes: the distribution of power as well as the exercise of power. Otherwise, we keep the essence of despotic governance intact.

As a result of this coincidence of the failure of governing regimes, as well as stagnation in governance reform, we have what we characterise as a state of anticipation and angst. I would like to describe it as the critical state of the Arab nation facing a historical moment in which one governing regime has failed and is in the throes of death, while a new one that is closer to our ideal of a society of freedom and good governance is yet to be born. This very complex state of anticipation and angst opens up to many alternative futures. In my opinion, it seems that while most of these futures are unacceptable or undesirable, some are promising.

## Scenarios for the future

There are in my view three basic alternative scenarios for the future of freedom and governance in Arab countries. The first one is naturally a continuation of the status quo, the present distribution of power, the present authoritarian exercise of power. We have figuratively described this as 'impending disaster', i.e. a continuation of the status quo would lead to disaster in our countries. The operative concept here is that when you have a failure in human development terms it would imply injustice suffered by people, injustice suffered at the hands of national governance regimes as well as at the hands of foreign powers occupying and violating the fundamental element of national liberation. When you suffer injustice and you do not possess peaceful and effective means of addressing this injustice, the situation results in hopelessness and despair, an explosive combination that ends up as an invitation to violent protest behaviour.

In my opinion a continuation of the status quo can lead to a stage of violent social conflict in Arab countries. We are seeing the beginnings of this catastrophic scenario in some Arab countries. Saudi Arabia could be one example as it could be the archetype example of the failure of development in a country that is supposed to be extremely rich, at least this is the illusion! Nevertheless, until the present day there are still pockets of abject poverty in Saudi Arabia, and there is a very high proportion of Saudi youth unemployed and suffering addiction to drugs and other social ills. Everybody knows of course that in the last two years we have seen flare-ups of violent internal conflicts in Saudi Arabia that could even get worse if the present situation continues. We are seeing similar beginnings of violent internal conflicts in countries like Egypt and Morocco, as well as in Kuwait which is another very rich country, and a country some consider to be rather free. So, I believe that it is inevitable to end up with violent social conflicts in many Arab countries if the present situation with the present distribution and manner in which power is exercised continues. Protests against present regimes have always linked failures on the national arena with failures on the Arab scale or the national liberation arena, and people recognise this link between failure at home and failure on the front of national liberation.

We have borrowed the French word *épanouissement* to describe the second main alternative. In Arabic the term is *izdihar*, and that is how it is used in the latest Arab Human Development Report. The operative concept here is that we need a redistribution of power, we need to build an institutional system of good governance and this has to be negotiated in a peaceful manner. However, for this negotiation to take place we need what we call an opening act, a beginning of a process of transformation towards a society of freedom and good governance and that opening act requires total respect for the key freedoms of opinion, expression and association. By freedom of association we mean two things: the freedom to assemble and the freedom to organise in civil and political society.

The condition of total respect for the freedoms of expression and association would result in a much higher level of participation through civil and political society. There is no reason to worry at all because Arabs suffer high illiteracy rates, etc., democracy as we know is an exercise in governance by continuous learning.

I believe this opening act of total respect of the three freedoms of opinion, expression and association is the only criterion for genuine governance reform. Opening up the public sphere through respect for freedom of expression and association would result in an automatic upsurge in participation that would be reflected in a much higher level of accountability of governance in the region.

It is very important to require that the three key freedoms be respected together, i.e. you cannot have freedom of expression alone and say that you have a free society. Freedom of expression without freedom of association, which is the situation that characterises our societies at present, is counterproductive. There is, at least in some Arab countries, some margin for freedom of expression but no freedom of association. And that is a very wrong situation that has to be changed if we want to end up with a society of freedom and good governance. Let me add here that our vision of good governance in Arab countries is not restricted to governance reform on the national level, it has to be complemented by governance reform on the regional level and on the global level as well. By regional governance reform we would like to see regional arrangements that can end up with integration, the European Union could be a leading example.

## Reforms on the global level

On the global level the most important issue is that the UN needs to be reformed in order to try to approach the ideal of good governance as defined above on the world scale. There are the two boundary scenarios for a future of freedom and governance in Arab countries: either an impending disaster or a human *épanouissement*. They are boundary conditions in the sense that they are extreme cases. Realistically speaking the future could lie anywhere in between these two boundary conditions. Here we recognise that at least one possible future can be realistic; by that we are thinking of what could come out of the G8 initiative (and I would rather call them the B-8, they might be big but they are not necessarily great; greatness should be based on moral superiority rather than power).

The G8 initiative for reform in the Arab countries is definitely less unacceptable compared to the US Administration proposal of a 'Greater Middle East'. It has been watered down deliberately to allow Europe to sign on to it. I believe the problem here is that the G8 initiative is showing signs of deterioration into an accommodation between the G8 and present (bad governance) regimes in the Arab countries. Their recent meeting in Casablanca was essentially a meeting between the G8 and Arab governments, i.e. the same regimes that we think have failed and need to be changed. The inherent danger is that the G8 initiative, if it takes the form of accommodating the present Arab governance regimes, will end up as an impediment to genuine reform, which calls for radical reform in the distribution of power as well as the way power is exercised.

## External versus internal pressures

There is also the problem of internal versus external pressures for reform. We recognise that there has been a reform movement in the Arab world but it has not been sufficient to attend to Arab aspirations for human development, freedom and dignity. So we believe that the way the G8 initiative is developing now could backfire in terms of impeding genuine reform towards a society of freedom and good governance. This is a challenge that has to be managed by the Arab reform movement. This is important since, in my opinion, it is inevitable from the way governance is structured in Arab countries – many Arab governance regimes derive their legitimacy not from popular support but from outside support – that there is going to be an element of external pressure for governance reform in Arab countries. We believe, however, that this external pressure has to meet certain conditions in order to succeed in producing the desired transformation in Arab countries.

First of all, this transformation has to be truly based on freedom for all. You cannot reform a country by occupying it and thus depriving its people of the fundamental right to self determination. There has to be a total respect of the international human rights law, in particular with respect to national liberation. There should be respect by outside forces for the fact that Arabs have to find their own way to freedom and good governance. There should be an effort to include all vital societal forces in Arab countries in the process of reform. We have seen before attempts at exclusion of societal forces, sometimes under pressure of foreign powers. Outside forces have to be willing to respect the outcome of free popular choice in Arab countries. They have to work within the framework of a partnership of equals anchored in mutual respect and understanding, rather than the kind of patronage approach that has mostly prevailed.

Let me stress the fact that we are biased to the rather difficult and sometimes seemingly impossible scenario of human *épanouissement* and we approach it in the latest Arab Human Development Report from the perspective of helping to *make* the future rather than just trying to *predict* it. But we also realise that what we propose in the form of our preferred alternative to the human *épanouissement* scenario is something of a pure type on which variations would develop in each Arab society.

This process of transformation toward a society of freedom and good governance will require an opening act which would start with a total respect of the three key freedoms of opinion, expression and association, all together. This is likely to open up public space in Arab countries which has been restricted tremendously and would end up creating a vibrant and vigorous civil society that would lead the process of historic negotiation to real civil power and build a system of institutional good governance.

However, in the Arab Human Development Reports we do not make recommendations that we believe are suitable for each and every Arab society. We think that each and every Arab society should debate these proposals, take them as a strategic vision, and decide what to do with them after placing them in the specific societal context.

## The Role of religion

Any meaningful analysis of Arab society cannot avoid the question of culture, and specifically religion – particularly Islam, being the dominant religion in the region. Our position, as explained in the second Arab Human Development Report was, in respect to knowledge, that Islam poses no impediment to the acquisition of knowledge. As a matter of fact, Islam was a major pillar in the building of a knowledge society during the zenith of the Arab Islamic civilisation. There is also, in our opinion, no contradiction whatsoever between building a democratic society and Islam. However, having said that it is important at the same time to recognise that Islam is subject to interpretation. There are progressive and enlightened interpretations of Islam as well as reactionary and regressive interpretations. Bad governance regimes have tended to support and encourage reactionary interpretations of Islam. Part of the transformation towards a society of freedom and good governance would end up in our opinion with a predominance of enlightened interpretations of Islam.

We take a similar stand on Islam and freedom. There is no contradiction in our view between Islam and freedom. Although Islam does not describe a very detailed system of good governance it has many principles on which – using enlightened interpretation and scholarship, or *ijtihad* – a system of good governance can be built. We believe that presenting any false contradiction between Islam as a religion – looked at from the point of view of enlightened interpretation – and freedom, is a big mistake and is incompatible with the view of the Arab people at large.

## Conclusion

You do not liberate a people by depriving them of national liberation, thus reforms must primarily be driven from the inside. This is the only way to have successful and sustainable reforms. If people share in forming the vision of the society they would like to live in then they respect it and they work for it. Nevertheless, we have governance regimes in Arab countries that derive their legitimacy not from popular support but from the support of outside dominant global forces. I can see, however, a potentially useful role for outside forces that are not empire builders but are genuine friends of freedom and human dignity throughout the world. I see them helping initiate this phase of legal reform that is needed for the total respect of the freedom of expression and association. But then allowing the internal reform dynamic, that is most likely to emerge, to take its course undisturbed or unperturbed. The question is: could Europe, for example, rise to that historical challenge of supporting freedom and equity and provide genuine friendly support to governance reform in the Arab world or not? I think Europe has to put its own house in order first so as to become a credible global player in support of freedom and equity throughout the world.

# Prospects for democratisation in the Middle East

RAYMOND HINNEBUSCH

Since at least the fall of the Berlin Wall and the 1991 Gulf war, pundits have been expecting the democratisation of the Middle East. They have generally been disappointed, but not because of any cultural resistance of the Middle East to democratisation. Rather, it is structural factors that need to be examined.

One reason for the failure of democratisation is simply that the indigenous authoritarian states are not, as naïve Western democratisers seem to think, "unnatural" or lacking in congruence with their environments. At the time when these states were built, the structural conditions for democratisation were unfavourable and the social forces that might have struggled for it were weak. On the other hand, the resources and techniques for authoritarian state building were available. As such, Middle East authoritarian states represent a *successful adaptation* to their particular environment; as long as their congruence with their environment persists they will remain effective obstacles to democratisation. However, as changes in it induce crises in the state, democratisation becomes one – but not the only – possible outcome.

## Authoritarian state building

### Artificial states

Unfavourable structural conditions were shaped by the circumstances in which the regional states system was imposed under Western imperialism – according to the interests of the West, not the desires of the indigenous populations: borders were arbitrarily imposed on and cut across rather than being congruent with local identity. As a result pre-existing sub-state (tribe, sect) and supra-state identities (Arabism, Islam) have persisted and continue to powerfully compete with loyalty to the state. A secure national identity is widely seen as a needed basis for democratisation; competitive politics may exacerbate social divisions if there is no such underlying commonality to limit conflicts over more mundane matters. In such an environment authoritarian state-building – the strong hand of a leader above ethnic or religious divisions – may be seen as the most workable solution. The importance of congruence between borders and identity for democratisation can be seen in the fact that democracy has worked best in those Middle East states, such as Turkey and Israel, where indigenous leaders were able to carve out their own territory, one more congruent with national identity.

An inevitable result of the forced fragmentation of the Arab world into a multitude of small weak states was that activists, colonels and intellectuals alike tended to give priority not to democracy but to over-coming this disunity. Hence, the main popular political movements – pan-Arabism and political Islam – have been preoccupied with identity, unity, authenticity not democratisation and where they have seized state power, state-building has often taken an authoritarian form, with the state seeking legitimacy, not through democratic consent, but through championing of identity – Arabism, Islam – against imperialism and other enemies. Little momentum for democratisation can be built up when the political forces that would otherwise lead the fight for it have been diverted into preoccupation with other concerns. In the West it was usually the case that the solving of the national problem preceded and was a precondition for democratisation, but in the Middle East that problem remains unsolved.

Another consequence of the way the states system was imposed was that artificial boundaries inevitably generated irredentism (dissatisfaction with the incongruence of identity communities with a claimed territory) into the very fabric of the system. This in turn meant that the new states were caught in an acute security dilemma in which each perceived the other as a threat. While amongst the Arab states the threat largely took the form of ideological subversion, where, for example,

Nasser's Pan-Arab appeal could mobilise the populations of other states against their rulers, on the Arab-non-Arab fault lines of the Middle East, irredentism has been militarised – issuing in the Arab-Israeli and Gulf wars, all of which were primarily over identity, territory and security. Insecurity and war has naturally fed the rise of national-security states hostile to democratisation.

## Weakness of an indigenous bourgeoisie

In Barrington Moore's famous aphorism: "No bourgeoisie, no democracy". A capitalist class is widely thought to be the powerful independent force that could extract democracy from the state or at least balance state power sufficiently to allow space for civil society. Whether the weakness of the bourgeoisie in the region is principally due to the pre-modern state's hostility to private property in land and to the accumulation of merchant wealth, or due to imperialism's ruining of local industries and reduction of the Middle East to a periphery (raw material exporter) of the global economy; or to the revolutions which swept away what industrial bourgeoisie existed in a wave of nationalisations – the region seems to be an exceptionally hostile environment to the growth of a bourgeoisie. Incessant war also deters investment while oil relieves states of the need to generate a favourable investment climate within.

One consequence of the lack of an entrepreneurial bourgeoisie ready to lead national development was that the working class, another social force that was instrumental in democratisation in the West, remained small. Another was that the military, being the best organised force in society, widely came to substitute for the bourgeoisie in the leadership of development; a consequence of this, in turn, was the wide preference in the fifties and sixties for statist economic solutions: the state would become the main entrepreneur and investor. One result was that the state took over or owned much of the economy, and people made dependent on the state for their livelihoods were deterred from demanding democratisation. Not only identity but also "bread" was put before "freedom".

## State-Building resources

Finally, the stuff of authoritarian state building was available. On the one hand, indigenous political association was readily adapted to authoritarian state formation. The historic strength of sub-state identities, rooted in an ecology fostering nomadic tribalism and reinforced by the region's mosaic of minorities, gave special strength to "small group" loyalties and politics. While the pervasiveness of such loyalties made it harder to construct broad based civil society or strong political parties, *assabiya* (exclusionary group solidarity) was widely manipulated by authoritarian state builders to construct solidary elite cores for their states. Moreover, the socialisation transmitted within the patriarchal family was arguably congruent with patrimonial rule at the state level: just as the father expects obedience in the family so the ruler does in the state. A kinship culture is especially compatible with the use of clientalism as a form of political linkage between elites and masses. But what has additionally happened in the Middle East is that *assabiya* and clientalism have been *modernised* by their mixture with imported modern political technology, namely the rational bureaucracy, the Leninist party organisation, corporatist syndical associations, and modern surveillance techniques. This has produced hybrid formations significantly more robust than their pure "traditional" or "modern" types would likely be. Finally the exceptional access of the Middle Eastern state to unearned outside resources – that is, "rent" – whether Cold War patronage (aid and cheap arms) or oil revenues, provided resources for authoritarian state building. Rent in the first instance was crucial to the construction of modern state structures and to the servicing of the clientele networks by which they coopted opposition and mass constituencies. Rent also meant the state enjoyed exceptional autonomy of indigenous society: it did not need a social contract, trading representation for taxation; rather, in an alternative sort of tacit contract, citizens traded their political acquiescence for economic entitlements provided by the state.

Almost all existing states took one of two forms, the *populist authoritarian republic* or the *rentier tribal monarchy*, and each was an adaptation to a distinct somewhat different ecology. Where there were major trading cities (with emerging modern middle classes) and large landed classes, generating land hungry peasant movements, middle class/peasant alliances formed against the landed oligarchy, giving rise to radical republics that demolished the class power of the oligarchy. Where nomadic tribalism retarded class formation and oil revenues became available, tribal-rentier monarchy survived. While the *origins* of these two regime types differed, in the process of consolidation they converged in terms of the strategies and structures of state formation. In both, *ruling cores* were build around *assibaya*: in the republics these might be recruited from the leader's kin or minority group (as, for example, the Alawis in Syria) while in the monarchies royal families were ready-made cores. In either case, democratisation would pose the risk that majority out-groups might mobilise against such in-groups. Elite-mass linkage in the republics was structured through party/corporatist organisation, while tribal organisation was a functional surrogate for this in the monarchies: in both cases, these linkage mechanisms were used to successfully construct clientele networks and to incorporate mass constituencies. Despite the ideological distinction between monarchy and republic, in both regime types public sector dominance of the economy (and of jobs) is combined with welfare state entitlements. In making significant segments of the mass public unavailable for mobilisation, mass incorporation in both regime types obstructs the formation of democratic coalitions (of possibly the bourgeoisie and lower classes) needed to extract democratisation from the state.

## Changing Environments: Authoritarianism under pressure?

All Middle East states have, to one extent or another, entered a period of on-going crisis, not least because they have encountered resource constraints (exhaustion of statist development strategies, the oil price bust) while, at the same time, their environment is being transformed around them. It is widely thought that, as a result, these regimes must change and, undoubtedly this is true at least in the long run. But democratisation is only one possible outcome: muddling through, collapse into anarchy, or adaptation through some limited liberalisation, are all possible alternative outcomes. Assessing how imminent change might be and whether it is likely to take the form of democratisation requires analysis of how far the former congruence of authoritarian states with

their environment has been undermined and whether the missing requisites of democratisation have developed.

According to *modernisation theory*, social mobilisation (education,
urbanisation, non-agricultural occupations) generates the *requisites* of
democratisation: e.g. identification with the state, demands for participation, the erosion of pre-capitalist culture, etc. There has undoubtedly
been a dramatic rise in requisite indicators such as *literacy* in the fifty
years since authoritarian state building began; as might be predicted,
political consciousness and activism does seem to have spread from
originally small middle classes to enlarged lower middle and mass strata.
Why does this not translate into democratisation?

One reason appears to be that the Middle East is still in the *intermediate* transitional band between low social mobilisation in which
democracy cannot be sustained, and the high levels in which authoritarianism cannot be sustained without escalating into "totalitarianism".
Democracy is, therefore *possible but not necessary*, and, as such, other
factors will decide whether it takes place.

One deterrent may be that because mass identifications have still not
crystallised around the territorial state and loyalties to sub- and supra-
state communities continue to powerfully compete with the state, political mobilisation threatens the state: mobilisation of sub-state groups
risks communal fragmentation while supra-state movements, notably
political Islam, condition loyalty on an Islamisation of the state that
many incumbent regimes cannot readily accommodate.

Political economy approaches stress class formation as a requisite
of democratisation. The expansion of the educated, professional white
collar middle class is indeed increasing what is widely thought to be the
keenest *constituency* of democratisation; yet it has not generally become
independent enough of state employment to realise its potential for
democratic mobilisation. The capitalist *bourgeoisie* has been fuelled by
economic liberalisation, and it wants political liberalisation of a sort
– access to decision-makers, legal protections for property owners, and
power sharing with the state. But it is also dependent on the state for
all the things – licenses, contracts, subsidies, monopolies – that make
the difference between riches and ruin. It is moreover, ambivalent about
democratisation since that could empower the working class and there

is a contradiction between the interests of the bourgeoisie which wants to roll back the populist entitlements, not least labour law, granted by the authoritarian state, while the masses are the main victims of populist rollback. This clash of interests obstructs the potential for the mobilisation of cross-class democratic coalitions against the state. Indeed, the authoritarian state has strengthened itself through cooptation of dependent bourgeoisies.

Given that the underlying structural forces are arguably relatively balanced for and against democratisation, the decisive factor that could tilt outcomes one way or the other would arguably be the *values and interests of ruling elites*. While the old generation of elites that built the authoritarian states were politically socialised in a period of democratic regression, the new generation of elites have been socialised in one of democratic advance and hence do seem to have lost confidence in the legitimacy of authoritarian rule and put more value on some form of expanded political participation. But whether they can act on that value change depends on whether they can find a road to democratisation that does not risk their position or the stability of the state. This depends crucially on whether elites can reach a power-sharing pact with the opposition or, more specifically, whether liberals within the ruling elite can reach an alliance with moderates in the opposition in order to marginalise the hard-liners in both camps. This, in turn, could provide the conditions for political liberalisation, if not democratic transition.

International factors have, on the face of it, appeared to shift the ground beneath the authoritarian state. Previously the superpowers provided financial aid and political patronage that fostered authoritarian state building and those authoritarian republics aligned with the Soviet Union, have, of course, lost their patron. Yet, US aligned regimes such as Egypt and Jordan, have suffered no comparable diminution of US aid despite the democratic rhetoric coming out of Washington which continues to pay them rent for their pro-Western foreign policies. More likely to be productive of democratisation are the partnership agreements the EU is building with local states which, though they stress economic liberalisation, seem also likely to foster a growth in civil society. Globalisation is ambiguous: it is widely believed to universalise liberal-democratic norms but others argue that in practice it *hollows out* democracy (removing strategic choice from the electorate). There is, moreover, an Islamist counter-globalisation which resists the triumphalist and increasingly intrusive discourse of Western liberalism and it seems likely to be intensified rather than diminished by a US "democratisation" campaign seen as a cover for neo-imperial interests.

## Roads to Democratisation

How do authoritarian states democratise? Democratisation has two dimensions which historically often come in separate stages: the first, at the elite level is political pluralisation which, as it deepens, is institutionalised in the "checks and balances" of a constitutional order; the other is the democratic incorporation of the masses.

If one looks at actual existing democratisation in the Middle East, two historical roads or models are apparent. "Consociational democracy", adopted in Lebanon, is a model for democratising a multi-communal society. It was arguably a product of unique Lebanese conditions: the mountains which deterred the emergence of a big landed class; the sectarian fragmentation which obstructed a strong state centre and army; the combination of this with Lebanon's position as a trading entrepot between the West and the Gulf, which allowed a bourgeoisie, in alliance with the traditional notability (zuama), to dominate and reach a cross-sectarian power sharing pact. The special circumstances of Lebanon make it doubtful whether this model could be transferred to other "mosaic" societies such as Syria and Iraq. Indeed, the Lebanese experiment collapsed, unable to carry the burdens put on its fragile architecture by regional conflicts; because these conflicts remain on-going, nobody knows whether its recently reconstructed version can survive the departure of its Syrian arbiter.

The contemporary experiments that became widespread across the region in the nineties, (in Egypt, Morocco, Jordan, Yemen, etc.) might best be called *"political liberalisation without democratisation"*. In all these cases, the president or monarch remains above politics and although he permits greater but still limited political liberalisation, he is invariably in a position to "divide and rule" the political arena, not least by using his tremendous patronage powers. These are hardly democratisation experiments because inclusion in the game is limited to the upper/middle classes, with various impediments erected against the political mobilisation of the masses. Hence, rule of law is advanced for property owners, but not to protect political freedoms; party pluralism is increased for the middle class, but if Islamists, speaking for those below, prove able to use the party system, barriers against their influence are erected.

Under the right conditions, either of these models could deepen into constitutionalism and mass inclusive democratisation. But what are the right conditions? The precedent of Turkish democratisation suggests what some of these might be. The Turkish state had a relatively secure national identity, hence the legitimacy to risk democratisation. Ataturk's relative depolitisation of the military meant officers saw themselves as professionals, no longer military politicians. A bourgeoisie had emerged from the ruling coalition itself, and believed democratisation would benefit it; the ruling party elite valued democratisation and knew the Kemalist state would survive it, since both regime and opposition shared core Kemalist values. Both ruling and opposition parties, having experience in party organisation, between them successfully included mass constituencies in the electoral process. Finally, international conditions were favourable: the democracies had triumphed in World War II, the US was encouraging Turkish democratisation, and (in contrast to the current period in the Arab world), Washington was seen to be on the side of local nationalism (supporting Turkey against the perceived Soviet threat). It is worth cautioning, though, that even in the Turkish case, democracy has proved fragile and when parties and movements speaking for have-nots or excluded elements challenged the establishment, repeated military interventions suspended democracy; although the military always returned to the barracks, it became the guardian of an elite version of democracy which conditioned democratic inclusion on public acceptance of elite-dictated rules of the game.

*Some* of the conditions facilitating democratisation in Turkey might be thought to exist in several Arab world cases, perhaps Egypt and Morocco; less so Jordan and Lebanon. But obviously they have not matured because in every case, the tendency is to view political liberalisation as a *substitute* for, not a *stage toward* democratisation; and every time the masses extract greater inclusion, we see democratic reversals, not deepening – in Egypt and Jordan – or, worse, collapse into civil war as in Lebanon and Algeria.

The conditions of failed or reversed democratisation suggest the importance of the *international context*. Lebanon's breakdown resulted from excessive external pressures from the Arab-Israeli conflict. Reversals in Egypt and Jordan were intimately connected with the *legitimacy problems* these states suffered owing to their special combination of separate peace treaties with Israel and close alliance with the US at a time when Washington was seen as the enemy of the Arabs and Islam (by contrast with the Turkish case). This deprives them of the national legitimacy which would allow them to risk democratisation; if they open space for political mobilisation, it inevitably takes an anti-American/ anti-Israeli form incompatible with their foreign policies and hence is reversed – for these regimes seem to value the rent provided by the US over legitimacy at home. Only if an equitable settlement for the Palestinians is reached and the Americans exit Iraq would American alignment cease to be de-legitimising. These cases suggest that democratisation under American conquest or pressure is a non-starter.

# US and European support to democratic reform: The intentions and practices as seen from the Middle East

YEZID SAYIGH

A considerable amount of rhetoric emanates from Western and Middle Eastern governments, multilateral international organisations, non-governmental organisations (NGOs), and intellectuals in the Middle East on the importance of promoting good governance, transparency, and accountability – not only in the sphere of delivering government services, but also in that of delivering political liberties, or democracy. But how can talk about purportedly abstract or universalised concepts – such as accountability and democracy – be translated into concrete policy and operational recommendations that are relevant to specific contexts with their political, legal-administrative, and constitutional legacies and social, economic, and cultural characteristics? This question is partly about transposing particular interpretations of these concepts derived from one subjective experience or perception to another – in which the promoting side often does not recognise its own subjectivity nor the context-dependent and contingent nature of its own historical experience. It is also partly about the interface between local and external actors, each of whom pursues a range of varying political, economic, and social interests and agendas.

This essay discusses the interactive relationship between the various parties with different – at times even divergent – objectives, both immediate and strategic or long-term. The interaction influences and ultimately shapes the development of government accountability and political democracy, at times promoting it but as often impeding it.

Take, for example, the case of Palestine, where an impressive range of outside actors – the main players in the international community such as the US Administration or EU, international inter-governmental or multilateral organisations such as the World Bank and International Monetary Fund or the UN Development Program, and international NGOs – have been pursuing since late 1993 the aims of peace building, security, free market economics, and democracy, frequently to contradictory effect. These strategic, value-laden aims have moreover been presented repeatedly by public officials, politicians, and academics as a basket of inseparable issues that have to accompany each other and fit together. That is not so true: the Palestinian case – much as others around the world, in the Balkans for instance – shows that the transition to post-authoritarian or post-conflict systems can be extraordinarily complex, difficult, and messy.

Reality shows that these strategic aims are often incompatible or contradictory, or simply very difficult to arrange simultaneously. At the very least, economic and political instruments deployed by outside actors to promote a particular political or social objective may complicate the attainment of another. Questions then arise, on the order of: should aid be offered as a 'carrot' or withheld as a 'stick'? Should political or technical issues be stressed? How should these and other necessary questions be debated and decided?

## Dilemmas and obstacles

Clearly there are fundamental dilemmas to be addressed, if the validity and feasibility of Western contributions to promoting government accountability and democracy in the Middle East are to be assessed. It is doubtful that these dilemmas will ever be fully or satisfactorily resolved, as they are integral to complex historical processes, but a necessary first step is to identify their constituent elements and dynamics and to explore what makes them problematic.

At the outset, I wish to frame what I see as a central question. The real concern that underlies much of the debate about democratisation and reform of governance in the Middle East – as indeed in any other developing region or polity of the world – is whether or not these fundamental changes of political structure, culture, and procedure can be achieved peacefully. Can democracy be promoted and attained without incurring the risk of violent dislocation and upheaval, and also without imposing agendas and objectives that directly threaten the core values, ideals, and autonomy of other peoples?

Furthermore, as Raymond Hinnebusch shows (see Chapter 2), the post-colonial governments that emerged in the Middle East were actually very successful in adapting to their environment, and therefore have been able to resist pressures to change and reform effectively and continuously. These governments reshaped their political, economic, and social systems to meet numerous challenges – whether of new ideological currents such as Arab nationalism, the Arab-Israeli and Gulf conflicts, the rise of oil wealth and 'rentier' economics, or superpower rivalry during the Cold War – and in the process were also able to deliver a lot to a significant number of their people.

Authoritarian politics was one consequence of neo-patrimonial systems of government, but another was a redistributive effect of wealth that meant that the Middle East experienced less income disparity than most other regions of the world, at least until the 1990s when the pace of economic liberalisation quickened. A further consequence is that political and governance systems in the Middle East have proven to be not only very resistant to meaningful change or to well-intended policy recommendations and exhortations from both domestic and external actors, but also to be incapable of changing themselves from within. The latter may be the more dangerous aspect, since it requires system breakdown for significant change to occur – with attendant risk of violence and of social and economic crisis – and suggests a much higher level of political contention and polarisation within society.

## The Palestinian and Kuwaiti cases

Palestine, which is an area of particular expertise for me, illustrates this dilemma. The Palestinian Authority (PA), established in July 1994 and headed by Yasser Arafat until his death in November 2004, was certainly far more liberal politically than the Syrian regime or economically than the Egyptian one, for example, and was engaged in a credible level of political and economic democracy. Yet its system of politics and government was so finely balanced internally, and held within such an intricate and restrictive structure of contractual obligations towards Israel in terms of economic activity, access to land and water, and of course security, that it was incapable of reforming itself. By March 2000 the professional opinion I submitted to members of the international donor community was that real change in the PA would only come about through a system collapse: this could occur through generalised public non-cooperation or disobedience, which however was unlikely due to the cantonisation of Palestinian population centres and to Israeli control over all roads and borders; or it would occur as the result of a massive external intervention. The latter is what happened: the Israeli reoccupation of the West Bank in spring 2002 effectively 'broke' the PA. It was at this precise moment that Arafat started to cede some internally-driven demands for reform, a positive process that was soon discredited and largely derailed when US President George W. Bush made the replacement of Arafat the purpose of Palestinian reform and *sine qua non* of the peace process and Palestinian statehood in his 'Rose Garden' speech of 24 June 2002.

Interestingly, Kuwait provides a second example of democracy promotion resulting from externally-driven systemic crisis or collapse. Following the Iraqi occupation of the emirate in August 1990, liberal social figures and significant members of the Kuwaiti economic establishment struck a deal with the exiled emir in Saudi Arabia: they offered reaffirmation of his status as sovereign and reassertion of the legitimacy of the emirate, in return for his promise to restore parliament, which he had suspended a decade earlier. The promise was met on both sides, though the consolidation of the US-Kuwaiti security relationship following the liberation of Kuwait reduced the emir's responsiveness to demands for further democratisation; several significant sectors of Kuwaiti society – women, the 'stateless' *bidoon*, and Shiites – remain bereft of the right to vote.

The question raised by these examples is whether reform of the political and governance systems in Palestine and Kuwait could somehow have been achieved more effectively – and more peacefully, in other words without need for such massive external intervention. More to the point in terms of my present purpose, could the international community that was so heavily invested in peace-building and state-building, have altered the course of events and outcomes substantially, by adopting different approaches or employing other policy instruments? In particular, could the US and EU, which had, and continue to have, special political and economic influence, have made a critical difference?

The Palestinian and Kuwaiti examples presented above are admittedly extreme, but many of the same problems and dilemmas of promoting democracy and government accountability arise in relation to the wider Middle East. An answer to the question raised above therefore requires me to highlight a number of obstacles of a general nature that explain the distinctive lack of democracy in the region, and especially in the Arab states.

## Political power and economic ownership

One issue in much of the Middle East is the lack of separation of political power and economic ownership. This has its historical roots and reasons that need to be assessed, much as the history of the rise of the modern state in Europe needs to be analysed in order to understand the specific nature and sources of citizen-based polities and democracy that finally emerged there in the 20th century. Of critical importance in the European case was the manner in which kings or would-be kings seeking to wage war – in the pursuit of territory or of suzerainty against rivals – had to negotiate access to material resources – money, arms, and men – with burghers, merchants, large landowners, and their like, and in the process created a habit of negotiation with other societal actors and of striking deals and balances and reaching compromises. At the risk of over-simplification, this was a major contributory factor to the ultimate evolution of democracy in Europe.

In much of the Middle East, in contrast, direct colonial rule gave way in the second half of the 20th century to authoritarian republican regimes or tribal rentier regimes. Consequently, there has been a high concentration both of political power – that subverted the need for democratic confirmation of popular consent and discouraged competitive politics domestically – and of economic power – leading to the cooptation of the would-be intelligentsia whose employment was secured directly or indirectly through the state sector, and of the would-be bourgeoisie which secured its business by entering into protected, parasitical relationships with the same state sector. Indeed, a key feature of most Middle East states is the limited development of autonomous social actors in general, not only those defined as middle class or bourgeois, commonly assumed in the social science literature to be prime movers in democratisation historically.

This helps to explain why we do not see a well-developed and independent bourgeoisie in much of the Middle East. The proximity between those holding economic ownership or access to economic opportunity on the one hand, and those wielding political and military power on the other hand, is so close that it produces crony capitalism at best, but little urge for real democracy, whether political or economic. The upper middle class, the 'big' industrialist and capitalist bourgeoisie in much of the Arab world has had little reason to emerge as the champion of democracy or genuine political liberalism. This is true even of countries where the free market exists, as for example in Saudi Arabia, as well as in previously semi-socialist Tunisia, Egypt, and Syria where the private sector has resurged, to cite a few examples.

Similarly, democracy emerged in Europe partly because the military were ultimately pushed out of power after they had successfully fought the wars that helped create centralised states. The new polities experienced a process of deliberate demilitarisation, the pushing back of the military and the civilianisation of power. This has not occurred in much of the Middle East since the 'independence period' of the 1940s and 1950s; the military remains a crucial pillar of power, and it is often closely fused with 'state managers' and ruling elites through political alliance based on mutual protection, joint commercial enterprises and economic activities (both licit and illicit), and marriage. This pattern cuts across boundaries, such as the former division into pro-Soviet and pro-Western camps during the Cold War.

### What kind of democracy?

A further dilemma is how to get the balance right between democracy ('real' democracy, whatever we mean by the term) and tyranny of the majority. Consider the recent, historic elections in Iraq: given demographic realities, even if the Sunni Arabs had participated there could still have been a crushing Shiite majority in parliament (assuming that most votes were cast on a confessional basis, which was not the case in fact). There are minorities of one type or another in every human society, but the particular, though hardly unique, problem in the Middle East is that certain communities find themselves in a 'minority' status when what is regarded by those in power as their defining feature – religious, ethnic, regional, or kinship (clan) affiliation – determines their access to, and participation in, the system governing the distribution of political power and other public resources. Whether the distinctions are formally entrenched in the system – as, for example, with the existing 'consociational' democracy of Lebanon or the emerging one of Iraq – or informally – as in Alawi-dominated Syria or Najdi-dominated Saudi Arabia – they serve as a reminder of the additional, adverse side-effects that may accompany transition to democracy of the 'one person-one vote' type.

As an example of the dilemmas posed by this question, consider the potentially perverse consequences of enshrining and protecting the rights of minorities – whatever they are and however they are defined – by setting special quotas for their representation and participation in political life, and consequently in the allocation of public resources. The Lebanese consociational system is structured in this way: the president has to be a Maronite Christian, the prime minister a Sunni Muslim, and the speaker of parliament a Shiite Muslim; parliamentary seats are apportioned strictly on an overtly confessional basis, while government ministries and agencies and all posts above a certain level in the civil service and armed forces are allocated according to an informal, but no less real, confessional quota. This may be one way of ensuring that all communities receive a share and have a stake in the system, but is not full democracy and, more importantly, has proved repeatedly since independence to be insufficient to preserve social peace and avoid civil war.

Yet consociational democracy is what is being constructed in Iraq, largely because the US Administration that determined the approach and set the normative and operational framework for the post-Saddam political system believed that the country is structured primarily along fault-lines between Sunni Muslim Arabs, Shiite Muslim Arabs, and (mostly Sunni) Kurds. Seen in this perspective, Iraqi democracy could only be built on a confessional/ethnic basis. From an Iraqi perspective, the incentive structure promoted by the US Administration is clear: organise as a Shiite (or Kurd, or Sunni) and elect a specifically Shiite (or Kurd, or Sunni) representative in order to acquire political power or influence and public goods. So, will it ever be possible in the future to create an Iraq where everyone is truly equal under the law, where 'one person/one vote' applies? Many Iraqis clearly feel that they can, and should, mobilise on social, economic, and political issues *across* confessional, ethnic, or regional lines: witness the fact that the Kurdish parties received more votes than the proportion of Kurds in the population would suggest, and that the Shiite parties received considerably fewer votes than the proportion of Shiites in the population would suggest. The political system that Iraq is now in the process of building is better than the Saddam regime, yet 60 years of post-independence consociational democracy in Lebanon indicate that what lies in store for Iraq's own version may be equally unsure and unstable.

In all cases, whether striving for 'full' democracy or accepting more flawed versions (from consociational to 'limited democracy' or polyarchy), the most problematic challenge is how, then, to create a culture of mutual acceptance and accommodation, of tolerance of difference let alone dissent, in which minority opinions and realities are legitimate and count in a meaningful way? To put this question somewhat differently, in 'operational' terms, how to develop genuine political pluralism: multiparty and parliamentary politics?

This takes me to a final obstacle in the way of attaining democracy in much of the Middle East, which by the same token offers a route to improvement and genuine democratic reform. Democratisation requires effective and empowered legislatures, yet in most of the Middle East the power, authority, and prerogatives of parliaments are severely proscribed, if not wholly absent. For example, Syria under President Hafez al-Assad and then his son Bashar – and even Iraq under Saddam Hussein – has witnessed regular parliamentary elections, but remains unquestionably authoritarian. The conduct of elections in Palestine and

Iraq in January 2005 was far more meaningful, in contrast, but even then tells us little in and of itself about the process, nature, and outcome of politics there.

## The role of parliaments

To my mind, a critical question is the nature and extent of powers exercised by parliaments, and the more subjective question of their willingness to wield and protect those powers. Few Middle East parliaments have any real ability to challenge government or to question policy, lest they be accused of questioning the president or monarch. In both republican, formerly socialist Egypt and monarchic free-market Jordan, for example, laws exist that make it an offence to criticise the head of state or his family; these are applied in particular to the press, muzzling it in effect. More generally, Middle East parliaments are largely unable to hold the executive branch to account – not least in the area of security, but on most matters of import as well – and cannot really determine budgets or hold the executive (and head of state or ruling family) to financial account. The preceding also underlines the fact that democracy involves much more than periodic elections; it is about an entire system and political culture cultivated over time of formal rights enshrined in legal institutions that implement and monitor those rights continuously, through transparent processes, and that can themselves be held to account on the basis of clear rules. The difference between a cosmetic parliament and an empowered one is an entire institutional, legal, and administrative mechanism that backs up democracy and makes it an everyday reality.

Both cause and consequence of the powerlessness of parliaments is the weakness of party politics. Simply put, why should anyone who wishes to participate in political life or pursue particular agendas look to a political party, when its principal forum for influencing or determining government policy is a parliament that lacks such capability? Why engage in parliamentary politics when becoming a parliamentarian generally means being unable to make a significant difference to anything? Hence the incentive, instead, to resort to extra-parliamentary means of mobilisation and pressure. Palestine offers a telling case of this logic: Arafat made it abundantly clear to his people that the parliament they elected in January 1996 could be contained, co-opted, and marginalised by him. Little surprise, then, that the Palestinian Legislative Council, which generated the highest expectations, consistently fared worst of all government agencies in public opinion polls. More damaging, ultimately, was that there was little incentive to form new, civilian political parties as they had little chance of being effective and building credibility among the general public; instead, existing paramilitary forms of political organisation and mobilisation, best represented by Arafat's nationalist Fateh and the Islamist opposition Hamas, were far more effective, and logical, in that institutional and political context. There were no parliamentary parties because parliamentary politics did not work.

## Western policy options and interventions

I will now address more directly the matter of Western policy options and interventions, and their likely impacts. I do not take the view that what the West does in the Middle East, in relation to democracy or otherwise, is necessarily bad or driven by bad intention; however, there are evidently problems with Western governments and policies, as there are with Arab governments and policies. Most governments have contradictory objectives and policies, but this is of particular importance when discussing Western efforts to promote both the normative goals of democracy and other more material agendas – such as general trade, arms sales, or economic liberalisation – in the region. This in turn gives rise to the tendency of Western governments to extol outward or superficial aspects of democratic process such as the conduct of elections, regardless of the substantive aspects of the process (such as the powers, or lack of powers, of those elected to public office), when it suits their purpose to demonstrate a favourable disposition towards the country or government in question. The reasons for such a stance could also extend beyond commercial and economic considerations, to include matters such as positions taken by the government in question towards strategic issues such as Iraq (1991-2003), the Palestinian-Israeli peace process, or the 'global war on terrorism'.

In the West the US Administration has a particularly bad record in this regard, compared to the EU attempt to address democracy and human rights in a more systematic, institutional way through the Euro-Med dialogue or 'Barcelona process', though of course the EU has also been accused (especially in the US) of subordinating principles to crass self-interest. In general, Middle East governments have to do little more than state a commitment to democracy and offer evidence of greater political liberalisation (or a slackening of repression and censorship), in order to receive trade, aid, and arms. Clearly, too, the major oil exporters of the region – the Gulf monarchies, Iraq, and Libya – are not in a position of need anyway, and hence the West has little economic leverage in such cases.

This relative 'blindness' is especially apparent in relation to the practice of Middle East governments towards Islamist opposition groups, both armed and unarmed. Algeria has offered a stark example since 1992, when the army – the dominant force in Algerian politics and government since independence – intervened to cancel the second round of elections after the landslide victory of the Islamic Salvation Front in the first round. The suspension of democracy and assertion of military rule was met, in effect, by a sigh of relief in the West. A more recent example is offered by Egypt, which is the second-largest recipient of US foreign assistance – including, ironically, considerable funds earmarked for democracy promotion. Despite having largely defeated the Islamic violence of the 1990s, the government has increased its repression of the non-violent Muslim Brotherhood at little or no real cost in terms of Western trade and aid flows, arms sales, or even political rhetoric.

But what options does the West have, concretely? After all, the evolution of democracy is a long, drawn-out and complex process that is shaped by many factors, not to mention the accident of timing and of personality of significant actors at particular moments in history. For external actors that are not situated in local contexts to direct events requires policy instruments that are necessarily blunt and difficult to use with precision – the offer or withdrawal of aid or trade, for example – even if such intervention can be morally and politically justified. Even where the West intervenes directly, as the US has done in Iraq, it is still dependent on local actors to construct a democracy that can put down real roots and survive beyond the external intervention. Furthermore, experience shows that governments are rarely able to ensure that the means they can deploy lead to the intended outcomes, as other actors, even much weaker ones, also interact dynamically with these inputs and seek to turn them to their own advantage or to adapt to them in ways that preserve their existing privileges and security. Efforts that seek to promote a particular social group that is seen as intrinsically disposed towards democracy and potentially capable of promoting it – such as the 'middle class' or NGOs – are often revealed to be based on simplistic, generalised assumptions about the nature of that actor or on inadequate information and a loose reading of local social, political, economic, and institutional realities.

It is not entirely unreasonable therefore, nor altogether without practical merit, that much Western effort to promote democratisation (in the Middle East and elsewhere in the developing world) is channelled into 'technical' areas such as security sector reform and training. This often arises because Western governments and their formal aid agencies, multilateral institutions (such as the European Commission or the World Bank), and some international NGOs find it difficult or even counter-productive to tackle directly such issues as security sector involvement in illicit commercial activities and the 'black' or 'parallel' economy or crony relationships between senior officers and state managers and their families. Instead, it is hoped that training police forces to be better at their job, including instruction in the law and human rights, will have a beneficial, if incremental, impact.

While the intentions are commendable and the effort worth undertaking in and of itself, the approach is no substitute for *democratic control* by *civilian government* over the internal security services (or armed forces). There are numerous examples of training leading to improved handling by the police of the general public and to fewer deaths of people in police custody – Jordan or the United Arab Emirates are among the more shining examples – but little evidence that this has altered fundamentally the nature and purpose of security sector activity, let alone affected the autocratic structure of political power in any meaningful way. Much the same could be said of other areas of technical assistance, such as training in parliamentary procedure, which though helpful and potentially contributing to democratic process is ultimately stymied if parliamentarians and parties lack the will or opportunity to exercise political will and acquire greater prerogatives.

A second Western approach is to channel aid towards advocacy NGOs working on democracy, human rights, women's issues, and so on. Yet once again the results are very mixed, at best. Egypt again offers a good example: the US directed some $800 million in aid towards Egyptian non-governmental projects and organisations in the broad field of democracy promotion in the first 18 years or so after the signing of the Egyptian-Israeli peace treaty in 1979. However, it would be difficult indeed to identify any tangible improvements resulting from this massive investment. This stark record is a reminder of the problem inherent in assuming that certain identified actors – such as the bourgeoisie or, in this case, NGOs – can take on the task of bringing about major political change. A similar problem arises when Western aid and development loans have been deployed to promote free market enterprise, in the hope that this will assist the emergence of an independent-minded and liberal middle class, which will pressure governments for greater democracy. Indeed, there can be adverse consequences, such as the transformation of the NGO community into a new business sector; this might seem an example of healthy entrepreneurship, but the price is the rise of a new dependency on Western aid flows.

Besides, economic liberalisation is not new in the Middle East. Even socialist-leaning economies in Tunisia and Egypt initiated trade liberalisation as early as 1969-1974, and there has been deeper and more widespread liberalisation throughout the region since the 1980s, and especially in the 1990s, including not insignificant privatisation in some cases. However, the process has also led to problematic results, not least increasing job insecurity and widening income disparity, a decline in literacy as well as in access to basic entitlements, and consequently the growth of the informal or 'black', parallel economy – all of which have undermined the drive to democratisation in a number of countries, where escape from the formal economy additionally means disassociation from the formal political system.

No less significant a consequence is that those who already hold political and 'structural' power or who have access to it are best placed to seize and benefit from economic opportunities opened up by the liberalisation of trade and capital flows. This is a familiar phenomenon from the transitional economies of Eastern Europe and the former USSR after 1989-1991: the apparatchiks become the new capitalists and the new political brokers. So too in Egypt, Syria, Algeria, Palestine and elsewhere, the elites and corporate sectors that the West expects to democratise may find this threatening to their interests as political and commercial entrepreneurs within an emerging crony capitalism. The response is often to engage in political liberalisation in its broader definition: loosening state controls over the media, relaxing security service surveillance and intervention, and allowing political parties to form. This has arguably reached the level of 'limited' democracy in one or two cases – Palestine is one, which is ironic since it is not even an independent, sovereign state – but potentially promising examples such as Yemen, Jordan, and Egypt have all regressed visibly from that level since the mid-1990s.

As noted earlier, Western options and approaches for the promotion of democracy in the Middle East (or elsewhere) need to be seen in the wider context of Western policy agendas in general. It is natural for Western governments, as for multilateral organisations and international NGOs, to have their own objectives and agendas. The problem, however, is that action by one of these actors may contradict, and hence undermine, action by another. A foremost example is divergent US and EU attitudes towards Iran, with the former effectively wishing for regime change and the latter seeking more modest aims, placing improvement in human rights and combating terrorism in the context of a 'critical dialogue'.

There are other, arguably more pernicious examples of contradictory purpose and consequences of Western policy. Possibly the most important is that the economic liberalisation so energetically pressed upon Middle East governments by the West ironically tends to undermine democratisation in tangible ways, largely because its intended beneficiaries are also its victims. First, economic liberalisation usually results in significant rises in female unemployment and poverty – as the state sector is usually the main employer of women, and their jobs are generally the more vulnerable during state contraction. Second, more broadly, 'strong' government is required lest the victims use the opportunity afforded by political liberalisation to mobilise against the government's economic reforms. Third, the cancellation or renegotiation on harsher terms of the 'social pact' between governments and poorer sectors of society creates a ready constituency for opposition movements, most notably the Islamists in the past two or three decades.

More noteworthy still is when different branches of the same Western government pursue contradictory agendas in the same recipient or target country. Typical is democracy and human rights promotion on the one hand, and trade and arms sales promotion on the other (often promoted by different departments of the same foreign ministry). Much depends on Western strategic or commercial interests that are served by the relevant Middle East government: from securing oil flows to securing sanctions against Saddam's Iraq or repression of Islamists in Algeria or Egypt. The example of Egypt has been mentioned previously – receiving over $800 million in funds earmarked for democracy promotion along with a much greater amount in US 'foreign military assistance', even as democracy regressed in the country. Palestine offers another: then US vice-president Al Gore congratulated Arafat on setting up state security courts, which were a travesty of democratic norms and civilian authority, even as USAID was funding technical assistance and training for the Palestinian legislature.

The flip side of the same coin is no less problematic from the perspective of promoting democracy: the 'carrots' offered by the West for this purpose may be outweighed by benefits accruing to recipient governments in the region from other areas of the relationship. This is evident in the case of the Barcelona Process, through which the EU promotes human rights and democratisation by targeting aid towards particular sectors, job creation, and so on. The problem is that from the perspective of governments in, say, the Maghreb, the $200-300 million they may receive over several years under the Barcelona Process is far less than the $2-3 billion that their immigrants in Europe may send back in remittances annually. The EU would have more success by reducing its own agricultural subsidies and tariffs and thus increasing the opportunity for Maghrebi agricultural exports to Europe, which in turn would generate greater income and job creation in the Maghreb and potentially allow local social groups such as farmers to gain economic and thus political autonomy from the state.

## Summary of options

I have set out a diverse range of issues affecting the process of democratisation in the Middle East, and emphasised the shortcomings and contradictions of Western policy instruments and approaches promoting that process. This leaves us with the two questions that have underlain this essay throughout: should the West in fact be involved in the process, and can it do so effectively?

Having adopted a critical view so far, it is fitting for me to stress my view that the distinction drawn between the 'external' and the 'internal' is largely fake, whether it is used by local nationalists to discredit and oppose Western involvement in domestic processes, or by outsiders who prefer to 'leave the locals' to deal with their own problems. Both positions are blind to reality: on the one hand local governments are happy to receive external (largely Western) exports, military assistance, and economic aid and are tied to the outside world in many material ways, and cannot credibly decry 'interference' when it comes to political issues and norms; on the other hand Western (and other) governments, multilateral organisations, and NGOs cannot deny the political, economic, social, and strategic impact of their extensive and multi-faceted involvement in the Middle East, and must take political and moral account. The question therefore is not whether the West should, or should not, seek to promote democracy in the region. This premise is false; rather, the real question is how the West can apply the principle of 'least harm' in its dealings with the Middle East in order to avoid inadvertently placing obstacles in the way of democratisation.

Of course, no matter how important or timely Western assistance and policy interventions are, they can only contribute to, rather than determine, the path and outcome of democratisation processes in the Middle East. The crucial role can be played only by local democracy advocates and reformers, who have to set the agenda generally, but who moreover have to be willing to stand up for what they believe in, even if this places them in the minority.

# Do Europe and the USA really want democratic reforms in Syria?

## 4

SAMIR AITA

## In the very beginning, there was democracy

The creation of the Syrian State took place within a democratic context. The French mandate divided this part of the old Ottoman Empire in different "States": Damascus, Aleppo, the Alawite and Druze States, in addition to Lebanon (Jordan and Palestine being occupied by the British). The Syrian leaders united their forces and, using the contradictions between the big powers, achieved independence in 1943 and full withdrawal of the French army in 1946. The initial democratic build-up was a result of the diverse nature of the Syrian population and political leadership. Not only did the elites of the major cities build alliances from the beginning with the regional nationalist leaders (Saleh Ali for the Alawites, Sultan Atrash for the Druzes and Ibrahim Hanano for the Kurds), but they also dealt successfully with their own major differences. Aleppo, the second biggest city in the Ottoman Empire usually views things much differently than Damascus, one looking towards the North and the other to the South. Discussions with the Lebanese leaders were also based on democratic principles, and the Syrian leaders accepted Lebanon as an independent State within its present borders as the best compromise.

The democracy of the incipient Syrian State was organised around two major parties (Al Watani and Al Shaab), representing the orientation of the urban middle class elites of Damascus and Aleppo, respectively. In a few years, they were able to make major achievements on both the domestic and on the international scene. Locally, they made strides in education of the poor urban classes and in development of the rural areas. The democratic spirit was also fostered by the birth and development of several parties, founded on new social backgrounds: the Baath, the National Syrian Social Party (NSSP), the Communists and the Muslim Brotherhood. State institutions were developed and unified, including the creation of a national army from the confessional militias established by the French. Democratic Syria became a founding member of the United Nations and of the Arab League, and quickly joined the Bretton Woods Institutions (1947)[2]. In Syria women had the right to vote before they did in France.

## Democracy meeting the challenges!

A few years after full independence Syrian democracy was challenged in 1948 by the trauma of the "Nakba",[3] the creation of Israel with the backing of all superpowers. A series of *coup d'Etat* followed. Two of these were related to oil interests as Iraqi and Saudi Oil pipelines passed through Syria to the Mediterranean Sea. Syria had also entered the era of struggle between the superpowers, at the very beginning of the Cold War.

However, a bloodless coup organised jointly between the political parties and the military elites, which had all agreed to overthrow authoritarianism, restored democracy in February 1954. This second democratic period was in many aspects unique in both Syria and the other Arab countries, and is still present in the collective memory.[4] Many Baathists, as well as one Communist and one Muslim Brotherhood member were freely elected. It brought major achievements in the development of the Syrian state institutions and the economy. The country became the first Arab country to create a central bank and to launch major agricultural development projects (the draining of the Ghab marshes and the development of the Euphrates and Tigris val-

---

2    To get rid of the imposed linkage between the Syrian pound and the French Franc.

3    "Nakba" in Arabic means disaster, referring to the "loss" of Palestine.

4    Memory reinvigorated recently in popular TV series, showing brothers and sisters, living under the same roof, adhering to different political parties and living the turmoil of this agitated cold war period.

leys). The industrial and financial sectors were also vigorously active and in 1956 the Lebanese often called Syria the "California of the East".[5]

Politically, the basis of the second democratic period was different. New populist parties emerged more strongly on the scene in an atmosphere of radicalisation that culminated in the active support to Nasser's Egypt during the 1956 Suez crisis and war. In this atmosphere, the populist parties were tempted, each in turn, to seize power directly. Concomitantly strong pressures were made by the superpowers to change the Syrian democratic regime. French and British assets were nationalised in 1956 due to popular anger against these powers for their attack on Egypt and for their support for the Israeli invasion of the Sinai. Syria also made a irreparable mistake with regard to the US when, following Israeli skirmishes and threats, it started to buy arms from the Soviet block and appointed a pro-communist chief of staff. This happened while the US was building an iron curtain – which included Turkey and Iraq (the so-called "Baghdad Pact"[6]) – against the USSR.

Foreign pressure on Syria culminated in 1957, with Israel and Turkey threatening to wage war together. This left no other option for the Syrian democracy than to commit a more than symbolic "hara-kiri". In 1958, the Egyptian President Gamal Abdel Nasser was offered a complete union of the two countries.[7] Nasser accepted the offer on the condition that all political parties were dissolved. The Baathists contributed to this rush, having their own agenda: to become themselves, as pan-Arabists and socialists, the party of Nasser in Syria, eliminating

5   Phrasing the qualification made by a US Agricultural mission in the Euphrate-Tigris valley where an extensive program of irrigation and crop development was implemented during this period.

6   The Baghdad Pact, signed in 1952, included Turkey, Pakistan, Iraq and Iran, Jordan attempted to join. Riots overthrew in a week the government that announced it.

7   A Group of Syrian officers headed by the chief-of-staff went to Cairo in January 1958, with no authorisation from the President or the Government, and offered the union to Nasser.

their strongest competitors – the Communists[8] and the parties of the urban elites – after having earlier eliminated the NSSP.[9]

However great his intentions, Nasser failed to govern the complex Syrian mosaic on an authoritarian basis and to maintain the United Arab Republic. The union was broken in September 1961, with the intention of restoring democracy. A small army unit, manipulated by the US and European powers, was able to crush the dream of Arab unity, because of a general discontent over the Egyptian officers' authoritarian ruling of Syria, and the elites displeasure over the nationalisation of banks and industry.[10] A weak and unstable democratic period followed in Syria for a year and a half, interrupted by many coups. The popular feeling was for the restoration of the union on better conditions.

## Decades of authoritarianism

The *coup de grace* to this unstable period came in March 1963.[11] A state of emergency was declared[12] and a new power system was established by a small group of army officers, mostly of rural background. All other parties but the Baath were quickly dismantled and their members persecuted. The elites of the big cities who had built the Syrian State were marginalised or forced into exile. Finally, even the founding political

---

8    The communists were persecuted by Nasser, and the head of the Lebanese branch, Farjallah al Helou, was assassinated savagely by the Syrian intelligence services during the union.

9    The NSSP members were tracked and jailed after the assassination of the Baathi deputy chief-of-staff, Adnan Al Malki.

10    The nationalisations announced in the last months of the union were cancelled, but not the agrarian reform promulgated in 1958.

11    Initially in order to restore the union.

12    In fact, the state of emergency law (law 51 dated 22/12/1962) was promulgated in December 1962, during the instabilities for momentary reasons (specific for situations of war and heavy turbulences). Military order No. 2 of March 8, 1963 declared an indefinite state of emergency. It is still valid (and used by the authorities) until now, even if it is in violent contradiction with subsequent laws and with the Syrian constitution passed by a plebiscite in 1973.

leadership of the Baath Party was itself ousted. It took the Baathist officers a few years to stabilise their new power system after fierce struggle between its members for control of all institutions, including a newly made development of the Baath Party as an instrument of control of the society. The confessional "assabiyah"[13] was widely manipulated during these struggles.

It was an anaemic and troubled Syria that went through the 1967 humiliation of the "Naksa",[14] leading to the occupation of the Golan Heights. Three years later another defeat followed during the Jordan-Palestinian "Black September".[15] These events brought about an end to the internal struggle, reducing the power system to a small and closed group around the late President Hafez Asad.

The authoritarian character of the new political system was asserted, leading to its "stabilisation". At the core stood Hafez Asad and a small group of family members and close collaborators. In the first circle, were the heads of the security services, of the elite troops and of the complex system to control the army, all directly selected and appointed by the core. In a second circle, the members of the regional command of the Baath Party,[16] the governors of the regions, and the heads of the regional offices of the party. A third and less decisive circle contained the members of the government, the army hierarchy and the state administration.

---

13  For the Arab Middle Ages historian Ibn Khaldoun, "assabiyah" is a strong common feeling shared by a minority group, which acts as a cement to make this group cohesive, in particular in the context of controlling and stabilising the power system of a country.

14  Word meaning defeat used to denominate the 6 days war.

15  The "leftist" baathist officers sent Syrian tanks to Jordan in support of the Palestinians. Many were destroyed by the Jordanian army, with the support of the Israeli air force. The Syrian Air force commanded by Hafez Asad did not interfere.

16  The election of its members was far from being "democratic" even within the Baath.

This political system was institutionalised by a Constitution[17] in 1973, placing all powers in the hands of the President and proclaiming the Baath Party "leader of the state and society". The remaining pan-Arab or socialist parties were outmaneuvered and divided. Some of their leaders were pressured into an alliance[18] with the Baath Party in a National Progressive Front (NPF).

This same power system was operative in Syria all through the presidency of Hafez Asad, and his son Bashar Asad inherited many aspects of it together with his position.

However, the experience of the 1950s has marked the Syrian people's subconsciousness, in the sense that foreign powers, and especially Europe and the US, have played a determinant role in crushing its democratic expectations, as well as their dream of Arab unity. This feeling has long contributed to the internal legitimisation of Asad's authoritarianism, as long as it holds the country united, stands up to the superpowers, and gives Syria a regional and international role.

## The spring of democracy?

Bashar Asad inherited this power system, after the death of his father in June 2000. Criticism of the abrupt change of the Constitution,[19] which was necessary to enable this inheritance, was mild. The new president was young and did not have a bad record, contrary to other members of the core power system. He had even supported some courageous calls for reforms in the previous years. Most importantly, everything was made by the power system, before and around the "biological hour", to ensure that there was no other possible alternative. The Vice-President, Abdel

---

17    The procedure for declaring a state of emergency in the new constitution was different from the one in the 1962 law. However, the state of emergency was kept on the basis of the 1962 law, and different special institutions (intelligence services, special tribunals) were created on its basis. All political prisoners (and even economic criminals!) were sentenced according to that law.

18    These parties, members of the Front, were until very recently not allowed to have any public political activities or newspapers.

19    Bashar Asad was much below the constitutional age for a President.

Halim Khaddam, was not even permitted to exert his constitutional intermediate presidency, until the – formal – election of Bashar.

In his inaugural speech[20] on July 10, 2000, Bashar Asad spoke of democracy, linking it to institutional development: *"To what extent are we democrats? And what are the criteria that democracy exists or not? Is it in elections? or in freedom of publication? or in freedom of speech? or in any other freedom or right? I say: In none of those... These rights are not democracy, but they are manifestations of its exercise and results of democracy... They are all built on the democratic thought, which is based on accepting the opinion of the other..."* Then he added: *"Consequently, we cannot apply the democracy of others to ourselves... We have to have our own democratic experience, issued from our history, our culture and our civilization... It should correspond to the needs of our society, and adapt to the constraints of our reality... Then the resulting (democratic) build-up shall remain solid, capable of withstanding quakes, however shaking...The destructive experiences are here (for proof) in neighbouring and far away countries".*[21] Asad presented the National Progressive Front as *the* "democratic" model best suited for the country, built on its own experience which, however, should be modernised and developed in harmony with Syria's new leitmotif of *"modernisation and development"*.

Whatever the interpretation of democracy given in the speech, the word by itself was repeated 16 times! This was enough to encourage Syrian intellectuals and activists to launch the "Damascus Spring". A famous petition (Charter of the 99) called in September 2000 for the end to the 1963 state of emergency, the release of political prisoners, the return of political exiles, freedom of the press and the right to hold public meetings. And this was followed by flourishing "salons" debating every aspect of Syrian social, economic and political life. One whole year full of rich debates before the regime cracked down on the most notable activists and thus put an end to this "spring". In an interview on the 2nd French TV channel, President Asad commented ironically that *"spring is not necessarily the best season"*!

---

20   Available on http://www.basharassad.org/english.htm (last visited July 2005).

21   Probably referring to Lebanon's civil war on the one side and to the collapse of the Soviet Union on the other.

However, the democratic movement did not die. Freedom of opinion and criticism developed, even in the government-controlled newspapers. New newspapers and magazines were published and tolerated. Activists launched several symbolic actions for political and social freedom and the regime has not completely returned to the practices of the 80's and 90's. Some of the trials of the political detainees[22] were even public. And representatives of foreign governments and NGOs were allowed to attend. Crackdown on opposition groups became random and rare instead of systematic, but remained efficient enough to create and maintain fear!

## Is "spring" really democracy?

President Bashar Asad was right that "spring" is not exactly democracy. In fact, the evolution of Arab countries, and Syria in particular, towards democracy, raises several issues that constitute the basis of a sustainable democratic development:

- political parties;
- the relations between the State and the power system;
- the positioning of the business community;
- and strategies toward Islam, and in particular radical Islam.

It is on this basis that one can analyse any democratic reconstruction in Syria, and frame the intentions and practices of the US and the Europeans to support democratic reforms.

## Are there any Political Parties in Syria?

Each democracy needs political parties to present government projects. Through free elections these parties will win or loose the support of the people, which again will lead to rotation in power.

In Syria, the Baath Party still dominates the political life. For decades it has created a system of efficient clientelism, where many young

---

22  Most of those jailed in the 70's, 80's and 90's did not see a court.

people, especially of modest origin, are forced to join the party in order to obtain scholarships, preferential entries to universities, as well as preferential access to public (and even some private) jobs. The party prepares its best staff to occupy key positions. Today the party counts two million members. It has internal elections, but they are far from being democratic.[23] The power system intervenes at different stages of the process to ensure the selection of loyal candidates.

Even the parties of the NPF cannot profit from such machinery, even if the limitations on their activities recently have been slightly eased.

The "Damascus Spring" did not lead to the establishment of a clearly delimited political movement, but it has shown, and still shows, the vivacity of Syrian political life. Its major contribution was to shake the operative scheme of the dominating political system. The critics did not only come from the so-called "intelligentsia", but even from members of the party itself. The Vice President, Mr. Abdul Halim Khaddam, faced fierce criticism from the Baath Party staff at Damascus University on February 18, 2001, for his and other Baathist leaders' abuse of power for personal (as well as their sons') interests. This "incident" was a major event, which significantly contributed to the decision of the power system to crack down on the "spring" in fear of a division of the party itself.

After the crackdown it was time to organise debates inside the party, allowing freedom to call for reforms, and involving external contributors, including some of the signing members of the Charter of the 99. Room was even left for calls to permit new parties and for an amendment of the Syrian Constitution, changing the Baath from "*THE leading party*"[24] of the country, to the "*government party*". However, the regime

---

23  The Regional Command of the party called more than a hundred party members, not elected by the branches, to join the last June 2005 Congress, and to be full members of the Congress, in contradiction with internal regulations.

24  Article 8 of the Syrian Constitution: "*The Baath Arab Socialist Party is the leading party of the society and of the State. It leads the National Progressive Front which works to unite the energy of the people to serve the aims of the Arab Nation*".

was not interested in precipitously convening the party congress,[25] which could have exposed different "currents" inside the party itself. In fact, not all party members approve of the take over by the "power system" of the party itself, and they have their own agenda. The opposition parties have been weakened by decades of systematic arrests and, following the end of the Damascus spring, by random arrests coupled with the slow liberation of long-held prisoners. For decades, these parties have been grouped, in exile, as a National Democratic Front,[26] but without being able to regain an effective backing inside the country. The most prominent leader of these parties, Riad Turk, head of the Communist Party (political bureau),[27] who has spent around 17 years in prison, was jailed again during the crackdown on the "spring", but soon liberated after overwhelming internal and international protests.[28] In May 2005 the party held its national congress and changed its name to the People's Democratic Party of Syria.

The Muslim Brotherhood Party has been in exile since the early

---

25 However, such a congress appeared urgent in order to change the by-laws of the party, placing "National Command" (representative of all Arab countries' Baath parties) above the "Regional Command" (that of Syria). And this is especially after the collapse of Saddam Hussein's regime, which has led to the categorisation of the Baath Party in Iraq as a "terrorist" party. The congress of the party was convened only in 2005, following Syrian withdrawal from Lebanon.

26 Since 1979 it has grouped the Arab Socialist Democratic Party, the Communist Party (political bureau) – that has changed its name recently to the People's Democratic Party of Syria – the Arab Workers Revolutionary Party, the Arab Socialist Democratic Baath Party and the Arab Socialist movement.

27 This corresponds to that half of the Syrian Communist Party which broke ties with Moscow in the 1970s and opted for Arab nationalism. It refused to join the National Progressive Front, criticised the entry of Syrian forces into Lebanon and denounced the authoritarian nature of the regime. Most of the staff of the party spent more than 15 years in prison, although it did not choose armed opposition as the radical Islamists of the late 70's did.

28 During his years in prison, Riad Turk became for Human Rights' NGOs the symbol of political prisoners in Syria.

80's, and its members are still sentenced to death in absentia.[29] During exile it has engaged in a dialogue with the other opposition parties on the basis of democratic principles. But even if it has even less freedom of action than the other opposition movements, Islamic identity reactions have spread in Syria again in the late 90's, as in other Arab and Islamic countries, and can potentially[30] sustain a large base of supporters for this party. Surprisingly, following the crackdown on the "spring", the Arab press on several occasions reported ongoing negotiations between the "power system" and the Muslim Brotherhood movement in exile, on the conditions of their return to Syria. But more recently, the movement opted for a democratic reform approach with the other opposition groups.

The NSSP took a different tactic and has now joined the NPF. Though forbidden in Syria since the events of the 50's, the NSSP never joined the opposition and its leadership in Lebanon allied itself with the Syrian "power system".

Finally, the recent period has shown the emergence of new leaders, and even attempts to create new parties. Riad Seif, a successful industrialist during the 90's, who became a deputy, and Aref Dalila, an economics professor, caught the attention of the system by their direct criticism of the "power system" itself. The parliamentary immunity of Seif was lifted after he wrote a letter to the parliament criticising the granting of mobile phone contracts without any license fees to the public treasury. Later, he was sentenced to 5 years in prison[31] for "trying to change the Constitution by illegal means". Others emerged as

---

29  Law No. 49 from 1980 sentencing to death whoever adheres to the Muslim Brotherhood Party, accused of having supported the uprising in several Syrian cities, including Aleppo and Hama, and of assassination of Alaouites linked to the power system (made in fact by a different radical Islamic group named "Taliaa Moukatila" – the combating vanguard). This episode almost ended by a civil war and with the Palmyra and Hama massacres.

30  Such potentiality is debatable, as the Islamic groups remaining in Syria are fragmented and do only have a local social basis, and the Muslim Brotherhood may have difficulties to federate them.

31  Dalila got 10 years.

human rights activists and are facing similar trials. Some groups also attempted to create new parties in 2004, for instance a "liberal party", whose founder after a few days of "tourism"[32] in jail was dissuaded by security services from doing so.

At the end of 2004, Syria has seen animated debates over a new law allowing the free creation and activity of political parties, with a view to the long promised congress of the Baath Party for official confirmation. The debates showed the necessity of changing the present constitution which does not explicitly guarantee such rights. Also, the parliamentary elections process should be changed, as it is not fitted for full functioning of the parliament on the basis of multiple political parties' representation and coalitions. Half of the deputies are to be directly selected by the Baath Party, as representatives of "workers and peasants".[33] And the recent elections have shown heavy implications of "interest groups" linked to the power system, financing the campaign of both "independent" or "workers and peasants" candidates.

The congress of the Baath Party was held in June 2005 after the Syrian withdrawal from Lebanon's strong impact on internal politics. The power system first tried to mobilise the Baath Party to defend its corporatist interests. As this did not work the President had to intervene personally to postpone the opening: no constitution change, no separation of powers between the Baath Party and the State, no principle of power alternation, no process of national reconciliation, no opening to opposition parties, and Muslim Brotherhood members shall continue to be sentenced to death. Heads of security services were also brought into the party regional command. The congress itself was preceded by a crackdown on the last "spring salon"[34] for free political debates.

---

32   After his release the founder of the party wrote an article in the press detailing the
     excellent conditions of his detention, which later on made another civil society
     activist write a sarcastic article about this particular "tourism".

33   Article 53 of the Syrian Constitution.

34   The board members of the "Jamal Atassi forum for Democratic Debates" were
     later freed, except one who read aloud a letter from the Muslim Brotherhood in
     a seminar where all political parties, including the Baath, made their statements.
     After the congress, the secret services asked for the complete closing of the forum.

Since the congress, the situation became tense on the issue of political freedoms. The Syrian blogs and websites announce regularly the creation of new parties. The "spring salons" and the unauthorised political parties defy the authorities,[35] and the consensus on the necessity of political reforms has broadened.[36]

On the level of political freedom, the 2005 congress of the Baath Party led to a stalemate in Syria, but there are more political debates than ever. The power system closed its scheme for reforms around a "Chinese model" with no political freedoms. The above described parties, as well as many others are proactive, finding new forms of mobilising popular support. Also, it is not sure that the Baath Party itself will in the long term accept being taken over by the security services, i.e. by the "power system".

## Is State and "Power" the same?

In Syria, as in most Arab countries, President Hafez Asad established a very clear conceptual and practical separation between the "power system" and the State. The circles of the power system are focused around the Presidency, which has its own logics of production, reproduction and control. The state is headed by a government, nominated by the President; the Ministers and the senior staff members have limited executive rights and autonomy from the "power system". The Regional Command of the Baath Party and other second circles of the power system suggest the candidates for government and for the major civil servant positions. The final selection is made by the Presidency according to different criteria: confessional and regional distribution, representation of the NPF, including a majority of Baathists and some "technocrats". The government does not rule according to any spe-

---

35 Riad Turk defied the regime in July 2005, by appearing on a satellite TV debate jointly with Sadreddine Al Bayanoni, head of the Muslim Brotherhood, sentenced to death.

36 See for instance the declarations to the press of the Syrian economist Nabil Sukkar, who for decades kept a strict economic approach for reforms.

cific programme,[37] even if Syria has passed several phases since 1971, very different with regard to their economic, social and political issues. Anyhow, important decisions are in the end taken by the power system, acting sometimes formally through the Regional Command, or on other occasions through the security services.

This system has not been established without resistance. In the early 80's, Hafez Asad was forced to cancel the non-political function of the Director of Ministry (senior civil servant who guarantees the continuation of the institution) and replace it by Assistant to the Minister, who can be changed at will. This was necessary in order to pass new laws and rules that were contrary to the logic and legality of the administration and the State. The Monetary and Credit Board for example, governing the Central Bank, was not formally dismantled, but it was for 20 years unable to arrange a single meeting; its deceased members were simply not replaced.

All state institutions have their counterparts in the Regional Command of the Baath Party, which have to agree on major decisions, otherwise the Presidency intervenes as an "arbitrator". As low wages and inflation deprived civil servants of any reasonable purchasing power, the door was opened for massive and systemised corruption. Those loyal to the "directives" were granted advantages in nature: free cars, travel abroad, etc. Key decision makers were allowed to take "illegal profits" from their positions, a fact which could be used against them (and was used on several occasions). This was of course valid also for the army, where the hierarchy was doubled by a security organisation, detaining the real power. Different army units were granted rights to organise contraband on a large scale.[38]

This situation guaranteed weak state institutions and concentrated the strength in the closed circles of the power system. It also weakened any possibility to apply the rule of law, as no coherence was sought in the judiciary system, as the judges experienced the same low wages and ensuing corruption as all other civil servants.

37  During the "modernisation and development" era of Bashar Assad, a tentative attempt to elaborate a program for the government through a debate between key analysts and actors failed, even if it was limited to the economic sphere.

38  In particular from and towards Lebanon.

As Bashar Assad rightly indicated in his inaugural speech, there can be no democracy without the development of institutions and without administrative reforms. But more than five years of his presidency has not led to any tangible result. The organisation of the power system remains untouched. Only one rule was introduced in order to change key posts, on the basis of age of retirement! However, it was not applied in many "difficult" cases. A decision was issued by the Regional Command not to interfere in government affairs. But in practice, the first and second circles still intervene at different levels.[39] The major change came for a period from the modifications of internal functioning inside the core of the system and between this core and the first circles. Ultimate power was no more absolutely detained by one man, but shared between the players, who can have different interests and stakes. The other main change came with a major involvement of power system players in business activities, with the attempt of each one of them to control and "legalise" a personal rent seeking activity. However, following the party congress of June 2005, the "old guard" was dismissed and the core of the "power system" became again concentrated around the President and his close family.

At the level of the State administration, young staff members, some of them Western educated,[40] were placed in different positions. However, no major structural reform was implemented, and no significant effort was made to raise the "official" wage level of key civil servants. Many of the "new guard" staff have already been involved in mismanagement or corruption affairs. The other "reformists" were invited not to challenge any of the rent-seeking activities of the power system, or even to integrate their business development in the "reform programmes".

The continuation of this strong separation between the power system and the State structure not only prevents a peaceful and democratic transition of power, it even contains the roots of the decomposition of the state, which is typical of the situation of "weak states".

---

39  And new laws were promulgated where Baath Party members were given roles in regulatory authorities.

40  In opposition to most Baathist staff educated in the former Soviet block countries.

## Where does the business community stand?

The historical Syrian business community suffered and lost confidence following the nationalisations of 1963, the dismantling of its political parties and the ousting of its relatives from the administration. Few linked their destiny with the functioning of the established state capitalism, or sponsoring and profiting from state purchase contracts. The majority went abroad where they prospered.[41]

In the early 1970s, Hafez Assad made a first step towards a handful of members of the business community, allowing them to invest with advantageous conditions in the tourism sector. And in the late 1970s, the same few had great opportunities to profit from huge public investments due to Gulf country transfers to Syria after the 1973 war. Similar opportunities were granted in the late 1980s for the barter deal with the collapsing Soviet Union, which led to a first broadening of wealth and capital accumulation.

However, it was in the 1990s that the business community prospered again: oil revenues, oil construction contracts, subsidisation of main agriculture crops, investment law No. 10, which transferred foreign trade from state organisations to the private sector, protectionism of local industries, contracts for the reconstruction of Lebanon, and trading with Iraq in the last years of Saddam's reign. All these factors have led to the development of a new wealthy and relatively large business community in the country.

However, this new business community did not ask to share power and/or to be directly involved in local politics. The complex and contradictory rules and regulations made it easy for the power system to crack down on any of its members for "illegal practices". Its most powerful members, and those who seized the original opportunities, are the direct relatives of the members of the power system.

In the early 2000s two groups clearly emerged. One, already powerful because of its direct links to the power system, sought to position itself in the most profitable rent-seeking activities: oil and gas, mobile phones, real estate, advertising, etc. This group favoured limited liberalisation of media and free speech, as long as it controlled such

41    Estimates of Syrian expatriates' assets abroad often amount to $US 80 billion.

media to defend its interests against even the official media, where some Baathists or independents might take leverage. Another group, the largest in number, has asked for the acceleration of liberalisation, the rationalisation of the administration and the equality of chances for all.

When foreign pressures are high on the country, both groups fear instability and position themselves against the pressures. And when life returns to normal, the contradictions between the two groups are sharpened and exposed in public. All groups, including civil society at large, are convinced that the liberalisation and political reforms are an inevitable outcome of the system. The first group linked to the power system as it is, is eager to gain time to secure its positions for such an outcome in the economic sphere, and to put its loyalists in key positions in the state structures. The second group is directly hit by foreign trade liberalisation, by the cumbersome administrative procedures, and, recently, by the pressures of the first group to take over its chambers of commerce and professional unions.

The largest (numerically but weakest in terms of power) group of the business community sees the establishment of democracy and the rule of law as a precondition to develop its business activities and investments. The takeover by the power system on rent-seeking activities is considered the major impediment to a better investment climate.

## Is Syrian Islam Radical?

Following the collapse of the peace process after Madrid, the UN sanctions on Iraq, and the US led invasion, Islamic feeling re-emerged in Syria as in most Arab and Muslim countries. This tendency to Islamisation was reinforced by the effects of liberalisation in the country, the spread of corruption and by the old and strong business links with the Gulf countries.[42] This tendency can be seen in the streets and the coffee shops, by the increase in numbers of women wearing "hijab", even among urban elites.

But however significant the awakening of Islam is in Syria, espe-

---

42   This has created what some scholars name the "Saudi era".

cially in cities like Aleppo,[43] the phenomenon is in no way as strong as in Egypt, Saudi Arabia or Jordan. Sunni in its basis, proud of the Shiite Hezbollah (who forced Israel to withdraw from South Lebanon), easily allowing mixed marriage between Sunnis, Alawites and Shiaa,[44] Syrian Islam still maintains its liberal Umayyad roots: All Syria, including the Sunnis of the cities, was proud to have the Christian Pope entering the Umayyad mosque.

The power system had for decades, however, used confessionalism and regionalism to justify its domination in fear of a supposed "overwhelming" Sunni majority in the cities. It has positioned itself as champion of the protection of the minorities and of laicity.[45] This major argument, publicly expressed in recent debates, is used now to postpone political reforms.

The identity of the Syrian population refers more to city and region than to religion. However, any democratic development in Syria cannot avoid the issue of political Islam, and has, at some stage, to launch a reconciliation mechanism covering the events of the late 70's – early 80's: the "civil war" or the "Hama and Palmyra massacres", thus enabling the development of an Islamic democratic political movement. The manifestos and debates of the "Damascus spring" did not evoke the "sad events", in a spirit of reconciliation and a global impulse for reforms under the umbrella of the new President. The "sad events" had the effect of a wound, a reason to move ahead. The power system did not use the same spirit of reconciliation to address this issue. Today publicly and in his discussions with US politicians and officials, the crackdown on Hama is presented as an early war on "Islamic terrorism", decades before 9/11. The temptation to continue using "asabiyyat"[46] as

---

43  Strengthened there by the feeling that Aleppo is neglected by the State based in Damascus.

44  Bashar Assad, himself an Alawite, is married to a Sunni woman born in Homs.

45  It is possible in Syria to find books critical of Islam, frankly secular or advocating new views on the understanding of Islam. Such books are not only banned in Egypt, but some are even prohibited in Lebanon, for confessional equilibrium reasons.

46  Several "assabiyah".

a mechanism of excuse and control is still extremely strong. The last congress of the Baath Party confirmed this, forbidding any opening towards political Islam. Just as the congress was closing the security services arrested several individuals accused of being radical Islamists. Earlier the same people would have been called "ordinary criminals". The "assabiyat" have however their own logic. Recently Syria experienced a strong awakening of the Kurdish identity, fostered by the developments in nearby Iraq and by poverty and social problems in the North-Eastern region. This is in spite of the fact that Syria has been much more successful than its neighbours in integrating the Kurds within its national and urban identities.[47] The problem has developed to a stage that forced the latest congress of the Baath Party to recognise some of the Kurdish claims.[48] Other clashes erupted between Alawites and Ismaelis in the coastal mountain region.

## US, Europe and the Syrian Power System

It is a commonly held belief in Syria that the US and European powers played a role in breaking their democratic experience from 1949 by having manipulated army officers to make their "coups". During the 50's and early 60's they are believed to have actively brought instability to the country, forcing it to make the union with Egypt without preparation. And since then they have supported all authoritarian regimes in the region.

Syrians have no confidence in the US, the strategic partner of the Israeli "enemy", and give no credit to it as an "honest broker" for a

---

47   In the 50's, several presidents were of Kurdish origin. The mufti of Syria, Mohammad Keftaro, was also Kurdish.

48   Hundreds of thousands of Kurds living in the North-Eastern region ask for Syrian passports, claim unfair treatment (land ownership, underdevelopment of the area, etc.) and have sympathy for the PKK and other Kurdish organisations in Turkey and Iraq. The Baath Party resolutions addressed the issue, without proposing a specific process of negotiations with the local representatives. The new economic plans of the State Planning Commission have focused on the urgency of developmental projects for the area.

Middle East peace.[49] Additionally, Syrians maintain a strong nationalist identity on both the Syrian and the Arab level, and they believe that the Western powers have been dealing with the Syrian regime only on the basis of direct interests. And since 1963 they have experienced strong variations in the relations between the superpowers and the regime. During most of the period France had better relations with Syria, especially as the US and Great Britain sided with Israel during the 1967 "Naksa", and after General de Gaulle's famous *coup de gueule* on Israeli arrogance, which brought about immense sympathy for France in all Arab societies. A period of favouring France followed; for instance the purchase of some *Caravelle* civil aircrafts in the late 60's. After the 1973 war, the relations with the US and Great Britain deteriorated significantly, leading to the freezing of diplomatic ties. In 1976 Syrians suspected a US and European green light for the Syrian intervention in Lebanon. However in 1980, the US listed Syria as a country supporting terrorism and, following the Israeli invasion of Lebanon and the dispatch of "multinational forces", relations with all the superpowers deteriorated further, reaching the level of limited military confrontation. The UK broke its diplomatic ties with Syria in 1986 on the accusation of terrorism.

The relations of all western powers with Syria improved drastically when Syria sided with the "international coalition" against the Iraqi invasion of Kuwait in 1990, and participated in the following war. This positioning of the Syrian regime was not popular, and was felt as a "sacrifice" in the hope of a full peace agreement with Israel, which could in particular lead to the return of the Golan Heights.

The relations with the US and Great Britain deteriorated again with the collapse of the peace process, and especially with the preparations for the invasion of Iraq. However, Madeleine Albright, Secretary of State, as well as President Chirac attended the funeral ceremony of President Hafez Asad in 2000 and indirectly endorsed the succession of his son. The invasion of Iraq made a new reshuffle of the positions. France and Syria sided together in the Security Council to prevent a UN resolution allowing the invasion of Iraq.

---

49    See CSS (Jordan Center for Strategic Studies) report "Revisiting the Arab Street, Research from Within", Feb. 2005.

It is worth noting that in 2003, following the US/British invasion of Iraq, the US Congress issued the Syria Accountability Act *"to halt Syrian support for terrorism, end its occupation of Lebanon, stop its development of weapons of mass destruction, cease its illegal importation of Iraqi oil, and hold Syria accountable for its role in the Middle East, and for other purposes"*. No mention was made of democratic reforms in Syria. Europe distanced itself from this unilateral US pressure on Syria, which clearly aimed to obtain Syrian support for the US invasion of Iraq. The Syrian authorities responded by a major opening towards Turkey and by accelerating the discussions for the signing of the Euro-Syrian "partnership", under the Barcelona terms. Some European countries siding with the US blocked the negotiations, for several months, in order to introduce stronger terms on weapons of mass destruction. In May 2004, George Bush escalated further by issuing an executive order:

> I, GEORGE W. BUSH, President of the United States of America, hereby determine that the actions of the Government of Syria in supporting terrorism, continuing its occupation of Lebanon, pursuing weapons of mass destruction and missile programs, and undermining United States and international efforts with respect to the stabilization and reconstruction of Iraq constitute an unusual and extraordinary threat to the national security, foreign policy, and economy of the United States and hereby declare a national emergency to deal with that threat.

Again, nothing on democracy for Syria was mentioned. The executive order included commercial sanctions. It was followed by a Department of Treasury note classifying the Commercial Bank of Syria, by far the largest bank of the country and responsible for most of the foreign trade financing, as a primary money laundering financial institution.[50]

---

50  Although it is common knowledge that the cumbersome regulations of the Commercial Bank of Syria can hardly allow it to launder money, and that the banks of some neighbouring countries are significantly involved in such dealings.

Shortly afterwards France abruptly[51] broke its "strategic cooperation" with Syria, and promoted the resolution 1559 of the Security Council on September 2004, supporting "free and fair presidential elections"… in Lebanon, as well as the withdrawal of Syrian troops. Syrian-French relations deteriorated substantially. However, the Euro-Syrian partnership agreement was signed in draft at the end of 2004. Syria agreed to organise elections for Iraqi residents on its territory and to make security arrangements with the US on its border with Iraq. It also went to Russia seeking re-establishment of "strategic relations",[52] canceling most of the old debts with the Soviet Union.

During all these fluctuations the Syrian population used to feel proud of Hafez Asad's foreign policy, as "he knew how to play it". This pride helped to accept his authoritarianism. The situation started to change after the collapse in 2000 of the last efforts to make a Syrian-Israeli peace-deal. The Basha-regime tried to play the same game. But despite the achievement of the deal with Turkey,[53] the Syrian regime is after the withdrawal from Lebanon more internationally isolated than it has been since the early 1980s. To the Syrian people the regime appears to have lost most of its regional cards and ability to interact "smartly" with international politics. The opposition hoped that this would bring the "power system" to an internal opening, seeking national unity in the face of adversity, but on the contrary, the congress of the Baath Party

---

51   This was especially abrupt considering that the previous year President Chirac in the Lebanese parliament had publicly stated his "understanding" of the Syrian interests in Lebanon.

52   A major step, which is leading to the draft of most of the old debts Syria had with the Soviet Union, leaving the country as one of the least indebted developing and Arab country.

53   The deal might even be shaky as Turkey still has strong military ties with Israel. Turkey and Syria have major common interests in preventing the dismantling of the unified Iraq and the creation of an independent Kurdish state there. Other reasons for the deal may be the internal difficulties of the Turkish ruling party with its other minorities.

in 2005 postponed the opening, reinvigorated repression, and called for "improving the relations with the US".[54]

## US, Europe and the Syrian political parties

As to political freedom in Syria, rights of free association and organisation of political parties, little has come during decades, either from the US or Europe.

The US State department issues yearly reports on human rights practices in Syria, where it is usually stated that:

> ... persons still in prolonged detention include members of the Ba'th Party, the Iraq Ba'th Party, the Party for Communist Action, the Syrian Communist Party, the Arab Socialist Union Party, the Nasserist Democratic Popular Organization, various Kurdish groups, and the Muslim Brotherhood. Scores of doctors, health professionals, and engineers have been detained without trial since a mass arrest in 1980, and hundreds of Palestinians and Lebanese citizens arrested in Lebanon and in Syria were detained without charge, although most were subsequently released.

The opposition parties listed in the report have little chance to get US support. Most are leftist parties. And during the Cold War era, no one could imagine the US supporting communist or socialist political organisations, as it is now doing in Iraq. And the State Department reports, contradicting the above where many parties were named, continue astonishingly:

> The Government uses its vast powers so effectively that there is no organized political opposition, and there have been very few anti-regime manifestations. Serious abuses include the widespread use of torture in detention; poor prison conditions; arbitrary arrest and detention; prolonged

---

54   And not with the European countries! Although such an alignment of the regime with the US is unpopular (see CSS report).

detention without trial; fundamentally unfair trials in the security courts; an inefficient judiciary that suffers from corruption and, at times, political influence; infringement on citizens' privacy rights; denial of freedom of speech and of the press, despite a slight loosening of censorship restrictions; denial of freedom of assembly and association; some limits on freedom of religion; and limits on freedom of movement.

Open US diplomacy did not make a strong case of defending political rights or political freedom, while it strongly pressured the Syrian regime publicly to allow Syrian Jews to emigrate or to end its support of the Kurdish PKK party. In its 2002 human rights practices report, the State Department did mention the crackdown on the opposition, discussing several individual cases, without presenting the dimension of the political movement of the "Damascus spring" opposition, and again no major public statement was made.

Everything looks as if the US has a problem with the very nature of the opposition parties and movements in Syria. This is the only thing that could explain the launching in the US of the Farid Ghadri Reform Party of Syria and its invitation to the State Department; that "party" has no backing in the country and no political credibility. The comparison was easily made with Iraq's Ahmed Chalabi, especially after Ghadri called for regime change in Syria by US military intervention. Nothing could be more efficient in removing all credibility from the US statements on fostering democracy in the region.[55]

The Europeans did slightly better. In fact during the dark decades of brutal repression, the leftist political activists who escaped prison mostly found refuge in France whereas the Islamists went to Germany and the UK (in addition to Jordan and the Gulf States). There were many public statements from the European parliament (EP) asking for the liberation of political prisoners, and Riad Turk, as well as others, were officially received at the EP after they had been allowed to travel abroad.

All these actions have not, however, reached a level of political dialogue with Syrian political parties or the "intelligentsia". No direct sup-

---

55   Astonishingly, one of the promoters of the liberal party joined the Ghadri move-
      ment and returned to Syria without being bothered by the Syrian security services.

port was given to these parties, and no direct pressure was put on the Baath Party. There was in particular no formal political work done by European political parties to assist the Syrian political parties to host and train their staff, weakened by years of repression, as they had done – not so long ago – with the Spanish or Portuguese parties during the repression periods in their own countries. There was also no systematic pressure on or dialogue with the Baath Party itself in order to develop more democratic practices. The ambassadors of Western countries, including the US, regularly meet in Lebanon and Egypt, the head of even banned political movements, and even the radical Islamists. There are very few reports of such meetings with Syrian political activists.[56] Rare were the conferences organised by foreign embassies in Syria on internal political issues, even during the "spring". No one took the occasion of the publication of the Arab Human Development Report, sponsored by the UNDP, to assist public democratic debates in Syria.[57]

Such interventionism in Syrian politics would have been difficult and risky. The Syrian political activists do not trust foreign Western powers, for the very same reasons as the Syrian population in general does not, and they particularly fear stronger repression when the authorities accuse them of "contacts with foreign powers", especially the US. And the US and European countries, as well as the EU, would also run a high risk concerning their geopolitical and commercial relations and upsetting Syrian authorities by making political contacts inside.

The Barcelona process could have been a good framework, but little was done. Even the Euro-Syrian partnership, which deepens Syria's involvement in the process, does not set any practical modality for fostering democracy in the country. Three articles symbolically refer to human rights and democracy, stating that "political dialogue" (i.e. between governments) shall cover such subjects (see Appendix 1, for the text of the related articles in the Association Agreement).

---

56  The Syrian Ministry of Foreign Affairs issued a note in July 2005 asking foreign embassies to seek authorisation before meeting civil society activists!

57  Only the Konrad Adenauer foundation of the German Christian-Democratic party, CDU, dared organise a symbolic meeting in Damascus to discuss the civil liberties issues that the report had raised.

In the middle of 2005 things slightly changed. The EU countries postponed the association agreement. The reasons were not clearly stated, and vary between the Syrian regime's continuous – i.e. also after the withdrawal – intervention in Lebanese politics, and the human rights record in the country. Also the US statements differ between "cheap regime change"[58] and strong pressures on the regime for its various policies, in Iraq (insurgents fleeing the border), in Lebanon (complicity in assassinations, support to Hezbollah, interventions in Lebanese politics) in Palestine (support for Hamas). But however strong the pressure, the Syrian population still sees no clear sign of Western commitment to democracy in their country.

## Who support the strengthening of the State?

Another indirect way to foster democratic reforms is to help strengthen state structures in relation to the "power system", or, more selectively, to pressure the "power system" itself.

For decades, the Syrian administration has received little assistance from the US or Europe. Most of the Baathist staff has been trained in the universities within the old Soviet block. There was no direct assistance from the World Bank or IMF, partly because of Syria's financial collapse in 1986, and the debt crisis that ensued until the end of the 90's. The authorities were also aware that "strange ideas" could be introduced with the assistance experts and it regularly advocated that Syria does not need foreign assistance, especially after its oil boom.

It is still inconceivable in Syria to receive US-AID assistance for either public institutions or civil society associations. The attitude is more positive vis-à-vis the European Commission, which has launched large assistance programmes for administrative and economic reforms (EC, by the way, advocates the same Washingtonian ultra-liberalism, fighting for downsizing the state). However, this experiment started too late, and is unlikely to produce decisive results owing to the complexity of EU procedures. More could be expected from direct state-to-state cooperation, as with the French assistance launched two years ago,

---

58    I.e. without military intervention.

which aimed specifically at administrative and judiciary reforms. The report on administrative reforms has been classified as "confidential" (!)[59], the one on the judiciary was still in process when the advisor to the President in charge of both files was fired (early 2005).

Astonishingly, pressures or sanctions from the US and Europe do not distinguish between the State and the power system. The trouble these commercial sanctions causes to the population creates adverse results: Complete cohesion of the population behind its State, and consequently the power system, and rejection of the unfair pressures and sanctions. A typical example of this is the Syria Accountability Act. The US administration chose to block exports of technological equipment for the internet, advanced health materials, electrical power plants, and to contain the activities of the major state-owned bank. All Syrians from the business community to the leftist activists considered such sanctions unfair. The sanctions were then rightly understood as an attempt to force concessions from the regime on the Iraqi, Hezbollah and Palestinian fronts, and not as pressuring the regime to work for a true democratic transformation.

The same negative reaction from the Syrian population occurred when France sponsored UN resolution 1559 on free presidential elections in Lebanon. The gesture of Chirac was felt as a betrayal. France has better ways to exert pressure, as most Lebanese and Syrian intelligentsia stated in *An Nahar* newspaper:[60] "The democratisation of Lebanon passes by the democratisation of Syria".

This refusal to separate state and "power system" in Arab countries looks like a nightmare in the light of the recent events in Iraq. The

---

59   Leaks indicate that the report stated that the administrative reform should start with the Presidential institution.

60   In recent years, the Lebanese *An Nahar* newspaper became simultaneously the major voice of Lebanese opposition to the hegemony of Syrian secret services on its political life, and, the voice for Syrian intelligentsia asking for democratic reforms. The phrase in italic is the title of a book by one of the main editors of *An Nahar*: Samir Kassir. In the last months, the debate went as far as discussing views of both Syria and Lebanon after the "withdrawal" from Lebanon. Samir Kassir was assassinated July 2nd, 2005.

Iraqi population suffered 13 years of hard sanctions because of their dictatorship. Then, when several hundreds of thousands of American and UK troops invaded the country to overthrow the regime, and to establish democracy (sic!), the first thing they did was to ... destroy the state institutions! The ministries were left to be looted. The army and police forces were dismantled. One could have expected that such state institutions, and the army in particular, were not happy for the disastrous outcome, but that they would have followed the occupation forces and later on the new regime emerging from elections if there had been stable security and living conditions.[61] Chaos was the choice of the US, and so was the awakening of all kinds of tribalism, confessionalism, regionalism, etc. What a positive democratic perspective for the population of neighbouring countries!

## Economic reforms before political reforms?

No democratic reforms could develop without a strong backing from the business community, which could see in these reforms a guarantee for the development of its activities, both in terms of economic growth and of social stability.

Significant economic developments and capital accumulation has occurred in Syria since 1990. The growth rates were high in the early 90's, due to oil revenues, but mostly due to the first measures of the authorities towards liberating ... business(!). The US and Europe[62] exerted pressure to negotiate Syrian debts multilaterally within the Paris club (while most of the debts were Soviet Union Military assistance). In the 1990s the Syrian business community sided with the state and the power system in refusing the economic "hegemony", and to gain time to obtain a step-by-step bilateral solution.

Growth rates decreased significantly after 1996 (becoming nega-

---

61   It could be argued that state institutions were controlled by Baathists, but this argument is not valid as it would have been easier, and politically more efficient, to have dealt with the Baathists in a democratic nation-building period in stead of the present situation of chaos and radical Islamist insurgents!

62   Mostly Europe, and especially France.

tive in 1999) and despite oil revenues they are still low due to structural problems of the economy: The absence of a friendly investment environment for the local business community as well as for foreign investment. The internal economic liberalisation was slowed down, favouring the members of the "power system".

US and European companies were, however, operating and investing in Syria. The biggest foreign company since the end of the 80's is … Shell, followed by Elf (now merged with Total). Both are extracting oil in the country and they have made large investments with the equipment and works mostly delivered by American and European contracting companies. Business, almost as usual! Certainly, these operations have their own Syrian "sponsors" who cannot exist outside the power system. Another example is car imports, which has also been a rent-seeking activity due to longstanding imposed import limitations. Dealers developed their activities, until a point where they were asked by members of the "power system" to transfer the agreements with the dealers directly to them. Many other examples exist where US and European export to Syria passed through a sponsor in the "power system".

The long-term outcome is, however, beneficial neither to the US nor to Europe. US companies have focused on oil while French and German companies concentrate on supplies to state-owned enterprises. When the State became less efficient, oil activities slowed down and Europe's share in Syrian imports decreased from 50 percent in the early 90's to less than 20 percent in 2003, as state procurements decreased significantly and the Syrian business community moved to import from … Asia.

Pressures from the US and Europe on Syria for opening up of foreign trade have led to the reinforcement of the "power system". The part of the business community it has created lives on rent-seeking activities and services (oil, foreign trade, mobile phones). It has no interest in fostering a democratic political development. By contrast, the early Syrian democracy was supported by productive, and not rent-seeking, capitalism in agriculture and industry. This is not a specific Syrian problem, it is linked to the basic issues of economic liberalisation and globalisation. What economic and social development does such liberalisation promote in third world countries? And does such liberalisation promote social groups which have an interest in consolidating democracy?

The newly-signed Syrian-European association agreement could offer a better framework, as it discusses in detail the rights of business development and the liberalisation of services, as well as the necessary transparency of state-institutions procurement. The other more productive part of the business of community welcomes a positive development in this field, with the hope that while bringing fair competition of European companies to the Syrian market, it will help them to obtain a similar fair competition in their own country. However, the examples from other Arab countries have showed that such association agreements have not helped the development of a genuine business community or of democratic practices. On the contrary, many have experienced the reinforcement of crony capitalism, so economic reforms are clearly not sufficient.

## US, Europe and Syrian Islam

The weakening of the state and the development of crony capitalism in Arab and Islamic countries has left most of the poor population without a perspective. This favoured the development of Islamic welfare groups and a return to Islamic values because of a general feeling of injustice. The return of religion is a worldwide phenomenon, which has to be dealt with as well in the context of international relations and the fight against terrorism, as in the understanding of local democratic developments.

Syria is located next to Turkey, where a democratic political Islam has now proved to be a reasonable alternative, even in the context of the aftermath of 9/11. The basic heritage of Syrian Islam (Umayyad) is also by nature secular. And social competition in Syria is much more between the major cities[63] and the cities and the countryside, than between religious confessions or ethnic identities (such as Kurds, Tcherkese or Armenians).

---

63    Damascus, Aleppo, Homs, Hama, Rakka, Deir Ez Zor, etc... This kind of Syrian
      identity differs very much from what is found in Lebanon for instance.

Europe, and especially France, has long manipulated the "assabiyat" in a way similar to the local "power system". From grants for studying abroad to immigration rights, Europe has long dealt with Syria within the framework of the "Question d'Orient". The elements of this framework are: Distrust of the Arab Sunnis, support for Kurdish separatism, "protecting" minorities and increasing its cultural influence amongst them. The US did not use this methodology until recently and it is more than symbolic to see that the two prominent universities in Beirut (where many Syrian elites send their sons to study) are: Jesuites Catholic Religious for the French, with mostly Christian students, and secular for the Americans,[64] with a majority of Muslim students.

However, US and Europe could benefit much from the peculiar secular nature of Syria Sunnism, and the strong integration function of Syrian cities. The country, in particular, harbours many Islamic doctors who are liberal-minded, and has Muslims developing theories on new interpretations of the Quran and the religion. Both groups could be helpful in neutralising the effects of the "conflict of civilisations" viewpoint, not only in the Arab and Muslim worlds, but also, and most importantly, in the West.

Whatever its practices, the particularities of the Syrian "power system" have led to the protection of secular thinkers, who developed their ideas on a Muslim and Arab historical background. Their values are strongly present in the education system and can be seen on bookstore shelves. For decades, the secularisation on the basis of an Arabic identity has created the union between the tens of communities of the country and it is the bedrock of Syria's national cohesion. The secular Arabs, like all communities, observe in horror the tribal and confessional outcome of the Iraqi "democracy". US and Europeans call now for the end of Arabism, and for the end of the "schizophrenia" of the Syrians, and push them to choose between their Syrian and Arab identities. A dangerous perspective for secularism, even if Arabism has been defeated in practice and if the concept needs to evolve.

---

64    It was, however, a Protestant college at the beginning of the 19th century.

## Conclusion and perspectives

Rhetoric in the US and Europe concerning Syria has only recently focused on fostering "democracy". The Syrian historical experience acknowledges that both the US and Europe have acted, as powers, in the collapse of its early democratic experience.

The country has undergone years of authoritarianism, with a build-up of a "power system" autonomous from the state. This power system withstood the transmission of the presidency from Asad father to Asad son. The little tokens of basic freedoms gained during the "Damascus spring" have largely been offset by the empowerment of members of the "power system" through rent-seeking business activities. In this context, US and European attitudes, positive or negative, deal with this "power system" as such and in many ways reinforce its position.

US and European support for democratic reforms should be ana-lysed in terms of the very issues which for the Syrians could effectively bring about such reforms: the development of political parties; the reinforcement and professionalisation of the state structures separate from the "power system", enabling the creation of a framework for democratic transition; assisting the business community to widen and sustain real productive – and not rent-seeking – activities, and maintain-ing the dialogue with all Syrian religious and ethnic groups alike, in particular taking advantage of the secular nature of Syrian Sunni Islam and of Arabism as a progressive identity.

Maybe Syrians are asking too much?

## Appendix 1

### References to democratisation in the Association Agreement

Preamble: "*Considering the importance which the Parties attach to the purposes and principles of the Charter of the United Nations, the observance of human rights, democratic principles and political and economic freedoms, which form the very basis of the Association*".

Article 2: "*Respect for the democratic principles and fundamental human rights established by the Universal Declaration of Human Rights shall inspire the domestic and external policies of the Parties and shall constitute an essential element of this Agreement*".

Article 6-1: "*The political dialogue shall cover subjects of common interest, and in particular peace, respect for international law and territorial integrity, regional stability and security, human rights, democracy and regional development, and shall aim to open the way to new forms of cooperation with a view to common goals, in these areas*".

# The crises in the Palestinian National Movement and the struggle for Palestinian democracy

## 5

GRAHAM USHER

## Introduction

Let me begin by saying what this presentation is not. It is not a historical account of the crises in the Palestinian National Movement (PNM). There is a strong case to be made that the PNM has been in crisis ever since its inception, and perhaps even before. Nor is it an account of Palestinian democracy. Palestinians have been fighting to democratise their movement long before George Bush discovered that the source of all ills in the Middle East was the lack of Arab reform (as opposed to, say, the expanding Israeli occupation).

Rather, I will be looking at the current crisis in the PNM and the current struggle for Palestinian democracy that has evolved out of it. In doing so I will refer to some of the themes raised in the previous chapters, especially the question whether external actors like the USA and the European Union help or hinder that struggle.

I will also be raising an observation of my own, based on my experience of reporting the Palestinian-Israeli conflict. And that is, within Palestine at least, the struggle for democracy is not a struggle between 'Western' democracy and 'Arab' autocracy. It is between two contending, though still essentially modern notions of democracy: democracy as a vehicle of imposed reform and neo-colonial containment versus democracy as an instrument for popular participation and national liberation.

## Causes

The causes of the current crisis are well known. The collapse of the Oslo peace process at the Camp David summit in July 2000 followed, in rapid succession, by the outbreak of the al Aqsa intifada. The containment of the intifada through Israel's military re-conquest of the West Bank followed, in rapid succession, by Israel's political unilateralism, realised through Ariel Sharon's separation plan and licensed by Bush's edict that Yasser Arafat and the Palestinian regime he headed were no longer "partners for peace".

Sharon's separation plan has two aims. The first is Israel's withdrawal from Gaza while ensuring that Gaza remains more or less permanently isolated from the West Bank. This was accomplished in August 2005. The second is the completion of the West Bank's separation barrier, which, depending on the number of settlements that remain "beyond the wall", will leave the future Palestinian "state" with between 53 to 90 percent of the West Bank, divided into four, non-territorially contiguous cantons, excluding East Jerusalem. This is what Sharon means when he talks about a Palestinian state "with provisional borders". Translated into Hebrew, it means the eastward, non-negotiated extension of "Greater" Israel with permanent borders in the heart of the West Bank.

Unilateralism requires that the Palestinian Authority be rendered redundant as a political authority and negotiator, with a mandate of resolving the Palestinian-Israeli conflict. This is what has happened. The PA's role today is largely civic: employer, service provider or security contractor for Israel's withdrawal in Gaza and ongoing annexations in the West Bank. It essentially fails on the promise Arafat made to his people when he signed Oslo in September 1993 – that the PA would be the nucleus of an independent Palestinian state in Gaza and the West Bank 'with Jerusalem as its capital'. This political failure is the basic cause of the crisis.

## Crises

It has several dimensions. It is a crisis of strategy. With Oslo, Arafat essentially mortgaged his people's aspirations to a strategy based on bilateral negotiations with Israel and an American monopoly on diplomacy. For Arafat it was a simple trade. In exchange for the PA delivering security to Israelis both within Israel and the occupied territories, he expected America to press Israel into a progressive withdrawal of the occupation.

With one or two glitches security was delivered, especially after 1996. But the occupation was not withdrawn. It was deepened. During the Oslo years, Israel increased settlement construction by over 50 percent (especially around Jerusalem), refused a third redeployment that should have given the PA 90 percent of the West Bank prior to negotiations on its final borders and institutionalised a permanent closure regime that separated Gaza from the West Bank and both form occupied East Jerusalem.

On the eve of the Camp David summit the PA had "civic and security control" in 18 percent of the West Bank, divided into eight disconnected enclaves. Israel had military control over the rest, with exclusive civic and security control in 58 percent of the West Bank housing the settlements, including their vast land reserves for expansion.

Barak's "generous offer" at Camp David did not fundamentally alter this system of Israeli control. Whatever the detail, most accounts of the summit agree that Barak offered Arafat "a de-militarised state" in around 90 percent of the West Bank, divided into cantons, with a mixture of functional autonomy and symbolic Palestinian sovereignty in East Jerusalem. For the foreseeable future, Israel would have ongoing control of borders, airspace and coastal waters. Barak ruled out any right of return for the Palestinian refugees other than a handful under the humanitarian rubric of 'family reunification'.

In other words, what in the West had been seen as a 'peace process' was for Palestinians Israel's latest mode of colonial dispossession. Camp David, in their eyes, simply confirmed the conquests set in place by Oslo. This is why for many Palestinians one of the very few achievements of Arafat's last years was his resolve to refuse it. He did – but it left his political strategy in tatters.

It is a crisis of leadership. I have been covering the intifada for the last four years but I still cannot tell you what it is for. When I asked Marwan Barghouti (Fatah's General-Secretary in the West Bank), he told me it was the Palestinians last war of independence. When I asked

Palestinian negotiator Saeb Erekat, it was about improving the Palestinians' negotiating position. When I ask ordinary Palestinians, it is about revenge – a 'natural reaction' to the collective violence of the occupation. When I ask Hamas, it is about forcing Israel's withdrawal without negotiations, a la Hezballah. When I asked Arafat, I never got a reply.

If he had an aim, it seemed to be to simply sustain the confrontation so that in the end Israel and America would be forced to return to him to contain it. But as the confrontation deepened, and Sharon and Bush rendered Arafat more and more irrelevant to its solution, Palestinians began to see his silence less as leadership than as powerlessness and, as the losses mounted, as a colossal abdication of political responsibility.

It is a crisis of governance. With the West Bank re-conquest – and Israel's siege and increasingly violent incursions into Gaza – the PA has collapsed as a governing, centralised authority. If you travel to Nablus or Jenin today, it is the Israeli army that rules and/or the Palestinian militias, led by many, controlled by none. The situation is the same in Gaza, but with one difference. There, a parallel Palestinian authority is emerging to fill the void left by the PA, with its own social services, political leadership and militia. That authority is Hamas.

It is a crisis of legitimacy. With Israel and the US' withdrawal of political recognition of Arafat and much of the existing Palestinian leadership, the PA lost its main source of international and regional legitimacy, since it was no longer able to bring peace. And through the PA's inability or unwillingness, or both, to control the militias, deliver public order and provide governance, it has lost much of its domestic legitimacy. By the time of his death, Arafat was not only irrelevant to Israel and the US. He had become irrelevant to most of his people.

## Reform

The current Palestinian struggle for democracy began the day after Israel's West Bank re-conquest. It was a spontaneous demand that became organised. It emerged with town hall meetings organised by Palestinian NGOs, became picked up by the younger Fatah leadership and the Palestinian Legislative Council, was endorsed by Fatah's Central Committee and finally – and only finally – by the international community, by which I mean the US, EU and UN.

Under this cumulative pressure, Arafat caved in. He ratified the PA's Basic Law after a six year hiatus, appointed ministers based on competence rather than loyalty (Salim Fayyad, at Finance, being the most obvious example) and agreed a 100-day reform programme whose end would have divested him of some of his executive powers. Then the reform process stopped. The reason it stopped I think says much about the US notion of democracy in the Middle East and why so many Arabs are resistant to it.

In June 2002 Bush predicated all progress in an Israel-Palestinian peace process on the Palestinians electing 'a new and different leadership ... untainted by terror'. It was followed by the so-called roadmap plan, authored overwhelmingly by the Americans, with no direct input from the Palestinians.

It spelled out what was meant by Palestinian reform: the creation of an "empowered" prime minister and new government separate from Arafat, "re-structured" security forces under American-Arab tutelage and the pensioning off of thousands of security personnel who also happened to be loyalist members of Arafat's Fatah movement. There was lip service to new Palestinian elections, but all were aware neither Israel nor the US would tolerate them as long as there was the risk that Arafat would be re-elected or politically strengthened.

In other words, reform meant regime change, induced from within rather than imposed from without, a la Iraq. But the means were similar: de-Arafatising the PA the way the Iraqi regime had to be de-Bathised. So was the objective: installing "a new and different Palestinian leadership" more amenable to Israel's security concerns, the American regional "war on terrorism" and perhaps a final or provisional agreement more in line with Israel's colonial ambition.

The Americans, through Bush's "vision" and the roadmap, hijacked the domestic Palestinian demand for democratic change and turned it into a means for containing the conflict and removing an elected, historical but insufficiently pliant leader. What they failed to see was that with such cooption the demand for reform became, in Palestinian eyes, an act of treason, and most Palestinians withdrew from it.

When, in March 2003, Arafat did agree to the position of prime minister and the other reforms demanded by the Americans it was no longer under the heat of Palestinian opinion. It was under duress of an external threat. Members of Quartet simply told him that Israel may use the 'diversion' of war on Iraq to do to Arafat what the US was planning to do to Saddam Hussein. Foreign dictates rarely lead to democracy – and they didn't here.

From the moment Mahmoud Abbas assumed the premiership he never quite lost the aura of being "America's man", a stigma Arafat was eager to apply. And when it became clear to Palestinians, and especially Fatah, that Abbas carried no more weight with Israel and the US than had Arafat, his days were numbered. Three months into his watch he resigned, and Arafat recouped most of the powers he had transferred to him. This did not change the basic view among Palestinians that Arafat and his autocratic system of rule were impediments to democracy. It simply underscored that so too were Israel, the US and the "international community".

## Elections

Has Arafat's death changed this? The short answer is yes, probably, at least in the short term. With Israel's "disengagement" from Gaza now an accomplished fact, Sharon's (or Binyamin Netanyahu, should he replace him as Likud leader) fundamental goal will be to complete construction of the West Bank wall and delineate the "security zones" as Israel's new, imposed eastern borders. What he and the US are now less able to do is veto Palestinian elections – local, presidential and parliamentary.

Within hours of his death – and despite reluctance by existing Fatah leadership – the PLC announced new presidential elections and re-confirmed that local elections would go ahead in December 2004, January and May 2005. It is unclear how much the US and Israel welcomed this. It was clear, given the momentum generated by Arafat's death, that they could do little to prevent them. The EU, to its credit, supported both presidential and local elections, practically and politically.

They may not have welcomed the results. On 9 January 2005, Abbas received the presidential mandate but with a 45 percent turn out and in the absence of challenges from Hamas and Marwan Barghouti, his main contender within Fatah (who, had he run, would be President today, say the polls). In the municipal elections, it was Hamas which received the mandate, winning 30 percent of all municipalities and 60 percent of all votes. But locally Palestinians were not voting about the final status issues or ideology: they were voting about governance, corruption and the credibility of the candidates.

There are further local elections in September and December 2005 and parliamentary elections, originally set for July, now rescheduled for January 2006. There is an overwhelming Palestinian consensus that the parliamentary elections will not be postponed again, whatever the fears held by Israel, the US and indeed parts of Fatah of a Hamas victory. There is also enormous Palestinian enthusiasm for them, and this I think for five reasons:

1) Elections will restore legitimacy and accountability to a Palestinian political system that has become bereft of both and provide Palestinians, finally, with an address through which they can again participate in and influence their own struggle.

2) Elections may unify and rehabilitate Fatah around a new, a more accountable leadership, enabling its necessary transformation from an inchoate movement to a political party with members, policies and elected leaderships. The alternative of course is that elections may fragment Fatah into rival factions but, should that be so, it will almost certainly lose its role as the dominant force in Palestinian politics.

3) Elections will integrate Hamas and, should it participate, Islamic Jihad into the Palestinian political system, rendering them more power politically but also more accountability over their military and social policies.

4) Elections will further de-factionalise Palestinian nationalism by institutionalising Palestinian politics, preventing the bane of unaccountable (and often minuscule) factions doing their own thing in the name of the "national interest".

5) Elections, finally, will shift the locus of Palestinian decision-making way from the historical leader and "leadership" to the people.

An instance of this can be seen with Abbas' promise that any final status agreement with Israel would be subject to a Palestinian referendum.

Finally, elections could become the forum for the long suppressed debate on the kind of final agreement with Israel Palestinians could accept as well as a referendum on the political, popular and military means to achieve it. It is already clear no Palestinian leader, including Abbas, will be able to accept another interim agreement or "Palestinian state with provisional borders" without at least guarantees as to what a final agreement will be.

In other words, elections could re-tilt the terms of the conflict back in the Palestinians' favor – away from the Israel/American driven notion that democracy is a means to strengthen Israel's security and integration/domination of the region and to the Palestinian and Arab notion that elections are one of the means that can be used to "end the occupation that began in 1967" and solve the refugee problem born of 1948.

This is where the two contending notions of democracy come in. It is not whether you are for Palestinian democracy (who is not?). It is which democracy you are for – democracy as an imposed "precondition" for sovereignty but whose immediate measure is the containment of the conflict in line with Israeli ambitions and American interests? Or democracy as a means, not simply to improve governance, but fundamentally to build a society necessary to strengthen the Palestinian capacity to resist.

That is the question, the dilemma. But it is not a dilemma for the Palestinians alone. It is a dilemma for us, here, in Europe, and those who speak, democratically, in our name.

# A Palestinian view on the role of Western NGOs in promoting democracy and especially women's rights in the Middle East

## 6

HANAN RABBANI

Dilemmas of democratisation are three words that summarise the key challenges facing both the Middle East and the International community as it seeks to formulate meaningful policies towards the region. In my essay I will explore some of these dilemmas. While my comments are of course inseparable from the broader political context, I will not directly address the Israeli-Palestinian conflict but rather explore the agenda of democratisation and its implications for related issues such as development cooperation, human rights activism, and the struggle for women's rights.

Democratisation has come a long way in the Middle East. It was not so long ago that the United States and Europe provided uncritical support to the most undemocratic and repressive forces in the region. In some cases, like Iran in 1953, Washington and London literally overthrew democratic regimes in order to replace them with dictators more amenable to their interests. Needless to say, such things were done in the name of freedom. In the Arab world there was not a single case of a democratic movement that was actively supported by the free world. Saddam Hussein, the Saudi royal family and Ariel Sharon were by contrast strategic allies to these governments.

If we move forward to 2005, one is perhaps inclined to conclude that things have changed dramatically. Even if Sharon is still a strategic partner and has been sainted by George Bush as a man of peace, one did not have to listen very carefully to Bush's state of the Union 2005 to learn that bringing freedom, liberty and democracy to the Middle East forms the core of US foreign policy. Indeed, the recent Iraqi and

Palestinian elections were presented as proof that this policy is already in full operation. Yet a closer examination of the Palestinian case demonstrates not only that this policy is, much as before, primarily a rhetorical instrument, it also demonstrates that even genuine advocates of democracy are as often creating dilemmas for their intended beneficiaries as they are resolving them.

## Democratisation of Palestine

Palestinian elections and democratisation are a case in point. The recent Palestinian presidential elections conducted by the Palestinian Authority (PA) were presented as a clear triumph for US policy. Yet the reality suggests otherwise. Until Yasir Arafat's death last November, Washington firmly and consistently opposed Palestinian elections. And it did so for a very simple reason; it knew who would win. Even after Arafat's death the decision by the PA to conduct presidential elections was hardly an American demand. The Bush Administration would have been just as pleased if Mahmoud Abbas had been appointed by a decree and ruled as an autocrat. It was rather in response to Palestinian public opinion that the PA, to its credit, decided to hold these elections. It was, to the best of my knowledge, the first time in history that a national liberation movement has chosen its leader by a popular vote.

But the real dilemma of democracy in Palestine today is that it is not being used as an additional justification for national liberation but increasingly as a pretext for maintaining the occupation. There is, needless to say, a world of difference between Palestinians who believe democracy is an essential component of a successful struggle to end the occupation and Israeli and American demands that Palestinians democratise as a precondition for independence. One does not have to listen too closely to Bush to conclude that to him Palestinian freedom means the right to conduct free and fair elections. Free elections are an essential component of democracy when the people have the right to self-determination and to establish their independent and sovereign state.

If the case of Palestine demonstrates that democratic advocacy can be exploited to deny people their basic freedoms, elsewhere in the region we see that agendas of democratisation are often informed – in reality misinformed – by ignorance and misrepresentation of the intended beneficiaries. To put it simply; there is a widespread view that Arabs – and more generally Muslims – are not yet ready for democracy. Their political culture, societies and religion – and therefore their citizens – are seen somehow incompatible with democracy and its values. As if the Arabs have inherited a gene in their system which resents and rejects democracy. Alternatively they are seen as so oppressed by their own culture and society that they are incapable of knowing what is best for themselves in order to achieve it.

## Arab women and hijab

The personification of these attitudes is of course better presented in the whole debate over the veiled Arab woman. As she is incapable of achieving her freedom on account of any combination of objective and subjective factors, she has to be liberated – whether she likes it or not – by those who know better.

This is the real dilemma of democracy in our region, and on this issue I would like to mention an example which refers to the imposition of the French law banning female students from wearing the hijab (veil) at schools in France. When the French law was announced, a strong reaction opposing the imposition of this law emerged in the Arab world. Interestingly enough a large number of the people demonstrating against this law were seculars including women's rights activists. Their reaction was based on the conviction that if we fight for women's rights and freedoms especially the right to choose, we cannot be selective. We therefore, fight for a woman's right not to wear the hijab in these countries with the same force as we would fight for a woman's right to wear the hijab has she chosen to do so. A woman's choice should be respected and defended whether she lives within or outside the Arab region.

## Western intervention and democracy

The last time Europe established mandates in the Arab world to prepare us for independence, we lost our country. Those who genuinely want to support democratisation in the Middle East should therefore support our agenda, not dictate it.

Democratisation of the Middle East has become a priority for Western countries and a prerequisite for any form of political and financial support by these countries. However, American intervention in the region and the double standards used in relation to the Palestinian and other issues which also extends to the new definition of democracy and human rights have made people in the region more resentful and suspicious of any Western intervention. At the time when democracy and human rights have become a dominant Western discourse in relation to the Middle East, many incidents prove that the American definition of democracy is very selective and dependent on its conformity to American interests in the region. In recent years this has resulted in a heightened tension in the Arab-American relations and more generally the Arab-Western relations which have suffered for decades from misconceptions and stereotypes on both sides.

## Image of the other

On the *Arab* side this is related to historical developments and political realities associated in the Arab minds with Europeans. These include:
1) Colonial history
2) Economic domination of the West which is often referred to as neo-colonialism
3) Political power and political interventions in the affairs of Arab countries

On the *Western* side, the image of Arabs has been influenced by the following factors:
1) Orientalist thought
2) Colonial history and the perception of the colonised by the coloniser
3) The power of Western media in its misrepresentation of Arabs and Muslims

## Development aid as a new form of colonialism

After long years of colonial history by Western powers in the Arab region which left deep scars in Arab minds concerning the perception of the West, a new form of domination has been demonstrated in the region, namely, development aid. Governmental and non-governmental support to Arab governments and civil society organisations has been on the rise in the past two decades. Foreign funding in the region is seen by many people as a new form of political and economic domination. Through certain policies and funds based on conditionality Western governments were able to interfere in the political, economic and even the social constructs of Arab societies.

## An example from Palestine

If we look at the Palestinian context for example we have a very active donor community, very interested in supporting certain governmental and civil society initiatives. Unfortunately, attempts to politicise this funding have been underway for the past few years. A very straight-forward example is the politics of the United States Agency for International Development (USAID) in Palestine. Funding by the USAID programme has increasingly become conditional: Support for any Palestinian non-governmental organisation involves checking the history of every person on the board of trustees of the concerned organisation. This investigation is done in search of any political or social links or connections to anybody involved with Hamas. So funding is conditional provided that none of the people who work in the organisation or connected to it in any form has any direct or indirect relationship with Hamas members. This is a challenging task, since Hamas, in addition to being a religious movement, is a social movement with widely spread charitable organisations and programmes.

It is not a clear cut situation and it is very difficult to draw lines to either prove or negate such connections. If one is not formally a Hamas member, one may still be living next door to a person who works for one of Hamas's charitable organisations. In another scenario, one of his family members could have benefited from Hamas's donations and social programmes.

In recent developments, USAID added a more extreme condition. This was devised in the form of a document denouncing "terrorism" that recipient Palestinian NGOs were asked to sign. This document had no clear definition of terrorism and did not draw clear lines between terrorism and resistance to foreign occupation. Without signing and approving this document, Palestinian NGOs are not eligible for USAID funding.

Active Western funding for initiatives and projects dealing with democracy, human rights and more importantly women's rights has been on the rise in the past several years. Work on these issues was very often represented as a condition for funding certain NGOs and certain governments' programmes in the region.

This interest and support should naturally lead to improvement of the quality of life for citizens in the region, had they been done out of genuine intentions and based on the needs of Arab societies. Unfortunately, the reality proves otherwise. Imposition of such programmes especially in cases where they don't fall under the work-mandate of some organisations, created greater resentment and the feeling that the donor community is trying to enforce uncalled for changes on the Arab culture. As a result, many Arab NGOs started implementing meaningless projects for the sake of acquiring the funds, and these projects did not leave a long lasting positive impact on the lives of women and other marginalised sectors in the society.

## A women's project in Palestine

I would like to give an example again from Palestine: in the late nineties, a big women's project dealing with protecting and promoting women's rights through legislation was implemented. It was funded by a European organisation. The initial assumption of the donor was that Palestinian women organisations would work on a project to advance their status and protect their rights in just fifteen months. In this context Palestinian women were enthusiastically working on this very exiting initiative for the first time in Palestinian history. The project created an open forum where Palestinian women would choose the kind of laws they aspire to have in order to guarantee their rights. The project, therefore dealt with sensitive issues including personal status law. It was based on the conviction that it had to be implemented with tactful awareness, great sensitivity in addition to a good understanding of the communities' needs and dynamics. If these considerations were not met, this project may end up delivering reverse results and drawbacks on the status of Palestinian women.

Unfortunately, those funding the project seemed less interested in the contents of project activities, rather they were more concerned to get progress reports indicating numbers and categorising participants into Palestinian Legislative Council members (PLC) and others according to their political and social status. In other contexts, rapid political changes in the occupied territories and the volatile nature of the conflict derailed implementation of certain activities for days or in the worst situation for a few weeks. The donor organisation was always persistent to have the activities accomplished according to the set timeframe with no consideration of the political situation and the importance of having conditions conducive to the success of activities. In the eyes of the implementing organisation, it was more important to concentrate on the quality of activities rather than the quantity. It saw it imperative to work on the type of information delivered and study the way it has been received by the audience regardless of their position, education or location. On many occasions donors reflect a lack in proper conception and knowledge of how to accommodate the funds and the time-frame needed in order to meet the needs of the target community. Donors seem to be fixated on implementing projects with specific budgets within limited time frames in order to list them in their achievement-reports in a specific country. Discrepancies and conflict between the donors' agenda on the one hand and the recipients' priorities on the other form one of the main challenges in development cooperation.

In the development terrain, donor-recipient relationship governs the relationship between north and south, east and west and in this context Arab-European and Arab-American relations. This relationship is unequal and unbalanced in many cases. It is based on misperception of the other. Furthermore, it is a known fact that in many development projects, an average of 35 percent of the funds is usually channelled back to the donor country through salary of expatriates, purchase of equipment and more importantly through consultants coming from the donor countries even when they are not needed and/or not familiar with the region, language, culture and the development context of the region as a whole.

## A project to establish two vocational training centres for women in the refugee camps in Gaza

Here, I would like to refer to a practical example I encountered in one of my jobs. A Western funded development project was aiming to establish two vocational training centres for women. These centres were set to provide training on basic vocational skills for women in two refugee camps in the Gaza strip. The project would in turn enable women to find a job which would help them make a living in the most impoverished areas of Palestine. The project took years to take off due to the bureaucratic systems of the donor organisation. Furthermore, one of the main issues that arose is the fact that the donor organisation insisted on bringing a women's expert from that country to carry out a needs-assessment study of the vocational skills needed by Gazan women in the refugee camps. Outside consultants are very important in certain development projects due to the expertise and knowledge they bring to the work. However, they were not relevant in the context of this specific project where even women in the West Bank would probably find it challenging to assess the needs of people in Gaza. This is especially true when the consultant has no knowledge of the language and no prior work-experience in any Arab country. This example reflects the fact that different mechanisms of work and contradicting priorities by donors and recipients can create tension instead of building up partnerships and good relations.

Gender relations, human rights and their impact on the well-being of women and their societies are very important components of democracy. Women's rights constitute an integral part of human rights. They cannot be discussed in isolation as rights of a specific social group in a certain context.

As stated in the Beijing Platform for Action: "The advancement of women and the achievement of equality between women and men are matters of human rights and conditions for social justice and should not be seen in isolation as women's issues. They are the only way to build a sustainable, just, and developed society. Empowerment of women and gender equality are prerequisites for achieving political, social, economic, cultural, and environmental security among all peoples".[65] Women's rights may lose their value and significance if taken out of the general context of human rights. Women are human beings; their position of being disadvantaged is inherent in a long history of cultural, social, religious and political factors worldwide.

## Women's rights and occupation

The starting point in this debate is the fact that in any existing society today one cannot advocate women's rights if the society as a whole is deprived of its basic human rights. This is accurate in the Arab world in general and more so in situations of occupation and war as is the case in Palestine and Iraq. A foreign journalist some years ago came to Palestine and was very interested in the Palestinian women's movement. So he came up to one of the women and asked her, "I do not understand what Palestinian women want? Do you want equal rights with Palestinian men?" The woman smiled and responded immediately, "of course not, Palestinian men have no rights".

In the case of Palestine, Palestinians as a nation have been and remain deprived of their basic rights to self determination, sovereignty, security and peace. The fundamental question is: Do rights for Palestinian women mean very much under these circumstances? Women's rights in the social context cannot be isolated from the political context. A Palestinian woman who has the right to education may one day run the risk of getting killed by an Israeli sniper while in her classroom, as has happened many times. Palestinian women may have the right to travel on their own, inside and outside the country, yet they cannot practice this right due to Israeli restrictions and check points. Pales-

---

65    Beijing Platform for Action, Fourth United Nations World Conference on
      Women, Beijing, 1995, Paragraph 41.

tinian women who enjoy certain reproductive rights according to the law could run the risk of giving birth at an Israeli checkpoint, whereby this right becomes meaningless. These examples indicate that rights under occupation and without self determination and sovereignty are meaningless.

Looking at the larger picture in the Arab region, despite the fact that women's issues and concerns differ from one Arab country to the other according to the political and economic structures of these countries, they stem from the same social and cultural systems which dominate the Arab world in general. Women in the Arab world remain marginalised in development and are excluded from the decision-making process. They are less advantaged than their male counterparts in almost all aspects of public and private spheres. Women's rights are often perceived as a Western trend and a foreign discourse. Culture, religion and social traditions are always used as excuses to justify the inability and reservations of Arab governments to advance the position of women.

This reality explains itself best when we study the position of Arab governments toward signing any international convention related to women's rights. This is especially true in relation to The UN Convention on the Elimination of all forms of Discrimination against Women (CEDAW) of 1979. Reservations of Arab governments who signed the convention touched the most important articles of the convention. In effect, these reservations make the convention invalid and defective. In this context Arab women suffer exclusion and discrimination in their own societies and experience double marginalisation when they retain the status of Arab migrants in the West.

At the level of NGOs working on women's issues, there are strong ties and joint projects implemented by Arab women's NGOs and funded by many European and other NGOs. Many of these efforts proved to be successful. However, the main challenge remains that Euro-Arab or Arab-Western cooperation at the level of NGOs is based on the donor-recipient relationship. If we are aspiring towards a real equal partnership based on mutual respect, exchange of experiences and cooperation, we should think of alternative models. I believe that as long as Arab NGOs remain dependent financially on European and Western funding it is not realistic to expect equal partnership. Room for manoeuvre should be created to provide guidelines for European-Arab NGOs to work on joint projects in order to promote clear roles and equal shares of decision-making power in the areas concerned.

It is important to note the existence of a dynamic women's movement in the Arab World. This movement started in the 1920s in Egypt and spread in different forms and levels to other Arab countries. Today, the Arab women's movement is adopting and advocating more than one school of thought. These include a genuine awareness and interest in women's rights as outlined in the international conventions and human rights' treaties, in addition to an interest in a new approach advocating reinterpretation of Islamic sharia including the Quran and hadith. In their struggle to protect their rights, it is true that Arab women need the financial support of Western organisations, but what they need most is Western understanding of their culture, needs and a space to decide and formulate their agenda in the developmental, political, social and cultural domains.

## Conclusion

Democratisation in the Arab world is a long and complex process. Like any successful struggle it can benefit from foreign support, but how such support is provided is of crucial significance. It must first and foremost be subordinated to the agendas of democrats in the region rather than subordinating the region to its own agendas. This is because at the end of the day only a process generated and led from within the region can succeed and endure.

# The limits of political reform in Saudi Arabia

## 7

MAI YAMANI

## The democratic charade

For many governments around the world today, the main challenge is to remain in power while facing competing, if not wholly contradictory, domestic and international demands. In this respect, Arab countries appear especially deficient. Infamously, the Middle East has the world's highest concentration of dictatorships. But this has hardly provided a recipe for stability. On the contrary, the region's dictators have proven themselves to be pathologically incapable of meeting either external or domestic demands for reform.

Is that now changing, as many observers hope? After all, pressure from abroad and the increasingly glaring legitimacy deficit at home have clearly fuelled growing interest among these rulers in learning to play the game of democracy. This year we witnessed the striking spectacle of elections in Palestine, Iraq, Iran, and Lebanon. Elections are planned in Egypt. Even Saudi Arabia – arguably the most repressive state in the region – has made tentative democratic moves.

Obviously, 'election' has become a buzzword for these rulers. But the term typically serves as a sort of talisman rather than representing a genuine commitment to public accountability and to free and open competition for power. Afraid of unleashing truly participatory politics, dictators rush to identify themselves with concepts selected from Western models but legitimised by 'Islamic' codes. In this way, they seek a political formula that can provide a patina of popular consent without threatening the status quo.

Saudi Arabia is perhaps the starkest example of this tendency. From the standpoint of the rulers, there are two reasons to hold elections: to comply with the demands of the international community and to buttress their crumbling authority at home. But elections mean something entirely different to the people, for whom the true significance of competitive politics lies in the extent to which real grievances might be addressed. In an age of globalisation and the free flow of information, the Saudi population knows that the rulers are inefficient, corrupt, and unable to provide effective leadership. The rulers, for their part, knowing what the population knows, are paralysed with fear.

In lieu of a new political strategy, Saudi Arabia's rulers justify absolutist monarchy with the argument that democracy is incompatible with Islam.

In contrast to the Saudi Wahhabi position, the majority of Muslim scholars, including the Sheikh of Al Azhar in Cairo and the influential Qatar-based Sheikh Qaradawi, believe that Islam is compatible with democracy. According to this interpretation, democracy is defined as respect for the rule of law, political equality among citizens, a fair distribution of wealth, an independent judiciary, and freedom of expression and assembly. To be sure, the right of citizens to a real choice of leadership, and the extent of elected representatives' powers, remains debatable and contentious. But there is nothing to debate for Saudi Arabia's rulers, for whom elections – or, more precisely, partial elections – do not mean a redistribution or democratisation of power. As both the rulers and the people are well aware, none of the democratic talk will change the fact that the country's fate – and its fortune – remains in the hands of a clique of octogenarian princes.

## External pressure points

Saudi Arabia's recent domestic moves are in part a response to mounting regional pressure, with the smaller Gulf States now competing in democratic reforms. Qatar and Oman have enfranchised women and established elected consultative councils. Parliamentary elections occur in Kuwait and Bahrain, and there is economic liberalisation in the UAE. At the end of 2004, Sheikh Mohammad al Maktoom, Crown Prince of

Dubai, recognised the full force of the popular desire for participation, declaring that Arab leaders must reform or sink.

The United States, too, has talked much about democracy, using it to legitimise its continued occupation of Iraq and, more generally, to portray itself as the liberator of the Middle East. But the US clearly is not concerned with resolving the real problems of the region's people, for it continues to pursue a selective policy that supports despotic regimes that serve its interests, with Saudi Arabia being the prime beneficiary.

Indeed, the US may attack the 'axis of evil', but it actively sustains co-operative regimes within the 'axis of oil'. Today, no less than before the terrorist attacks of September 11th, 2001, America's support for the Saudi regime is not conditional on democracy, but on the secure flow of oil. If the US administration cares at all about elections and democracy in Saudi Arabia, it does so only to the extent that such reforms help to sustain Americans' support for their governments close bilateral relationship with the homeland of most of the September 11th attackers.

Nevertheless, US talk of democracy raises popular expectations and places intense pressure on authoritarian regimes. The more these regimes talk about democracy with no tangible results, the more anger and frustration there is among the population. This anger is often channelled into expressions of anti-American sentiment, but it is ultimately directed against the regimes themselves.

## Elections without voters

Saudi Arabia's rulers, feeling that the country's status as the dominant regional power was in jeopardy, believed that they had joined the race for reform by staging municipal elections to consultative bodies, beginning in early 2005. Half the all-male membership of these bodies was appointed, and the female population was barred from voting. Nevertheless, the government described the elections as the dawn of a 'new political era'.

Women were excluded from the elections in line with the regime's embrace of the Wahhabi religious definition of activities that are compatible with the 'nature of women'. There is some disagreement among the princes, however. Mansour bin Mitib, the prince in charge of the General Committee for municipal elections, has said that the exclusion of women reflected the novelty of elections in Saudi Arabia, and that more time is needed for preparation. But while he hopes that women will be able to vote in 2009, Prince Naif, the Minister of Interior, will have the final word, and he says that women will never be permitted to participate.

The exclusion of women – as both candidates and voters – from the recent election has provoked international criticism. Nowhere else in the world has either Islam or dictatorship enforced the total and permanent exclusion of women from political life. In fact, disenfranchisement of women is uncommon even in most Muslim and Arab countries that hold elections. This point was hardly lost on Saudi voters, as televised coverage of Afghan, Palestinian, Iraqi, Lebanese, and Iranian elections has made universal suffrage a visible reality.

The first Saudi election was held in the capital, Riyadh, on February 10th. The second stage took place in the oil-rich Eastern region and the southern Asir region on March 2nd. The third and final stage took place in Mecca and Medina, in the Hijaz (or the 'Western' region as the Saudi authorities refer to it), and in al Jouf, the Northern Region, on April 21st.

The General Committee overseeing the elections was advised by the German Foundation for Technical Co-operation and the UN Organisation Team, giving the vote a veneer of international legitimacy. But a prince was appointed as chairman of the Committee, and, indeed, the control of the princes in all positions of power was reasserted, undermining any hope of broadening the scope of political participation.

The population understood this – and voted with its feet. Turnout among the Shi'a minority in the Eastern province was relatively high, with 16,000 registering in the small city of Qatif and the website www.rasid.com revealing far more enthusiasm about the idea of voting among the Shi'a than among the Sunni majority. In Riyadh, a city of 2.5-3 million, only 150,000 of the 500,000 eligible voters registered.

Overall turnout was low despite a series of campaigns led by Crown Prince (now king) Abdullah. Then again, the government, fearing the development of an electoral culture, did not necessarily want a high level of participation. Although low turnout is embarrassing, it can also be used to suggest to Western audiences that the population is satisfied with the status quo.

Moreover, it is widely believed that the rulers encouraged Islamists to participate in order to propagate the idea that fully competitive elections carry the threat of an extremist takeover. The message was both simple – "We have controlled elections in order to protect the country; ask for more and you don't know what you will get" – and effective. Indeed, the candidates who won in Riyadh and in Jeddah were Wahhabi Islamists, a victory tailor-made to worry the US about pushing for more democracy.

But the idea that Saudis yearn for nothing more than to elect their tyrants is a myth. Most Saudis are not Wahhabi extremists; in fact, the Wahhabis have always been a minority in the country.

Saudi intellectuals attribute the limited electoral turnout, more plausibly, to the lack of freedom of expression and assembly in the country, which frustrates real political participation. For example, leading reformists were jailed in March 2004 – and released only well after the elections – for signing a petition asking for a constitutional monarchy. Unsurprisingly, such episodes merely reinforce the public's lack of trust in the government's agenda.

## The mirage of participation

Elections cannot be separated from constitutional reform, despite the government's efforts to uphold such a distinction. The most crucial question concerns reform of the majlis al-shura, or consultative council. Can it become a real parliament? Would it be elected, and, if so, who would do the electing?

Currently, the King appoints the members of the majlis. They do not legislate, and they rarely even propose legislation. Instead, the King proposes and they approve. The majlis cannot debate the budget or military deals, nor can it question the financial allocation to the princes.

The late King Fahd announced in January 2005 that the number of members of al-shura will be increased from 120 to 150, but the responsibilities that they will hold remain vague. In the absence of constitutional reform, the fact that thirty more people get to sit in a room and talk without consequence will bring neither political stability nor social peace.

Similarly, Abdullah established an official 'King Abdul Aziz Centre for National Dialogue' last year as an acknowledgement of pluralism and diversity, with the country's main religious sects – Salafis (Wahhabis), Sufis, and Shi'a – gathering for the first time. But National Dialogue meetings resulted in discussions that have not been legitimised by the religious authorities, so nothing has changed in everyday life: the Shi'a still cannot practice their religious rituals, be witnesses in court, or even work as butchers, because the Wahhabis consider them heretics and apostates. As a result, marginalisation and exclusion continue to prevail over any hope of greater freedom and transparency, while the National Dialogue itself, having become utterly divorced from domestic reality, has turned into a propaganda centre whose participants believe that they are part of the state's message to the outside world.

Indeed, the National Dialogue has since been transformed by officials into an 'intellectual encounter'. Its last meeting, called 'Encounter with the young: reality and aspirations', resulted in a procession of grand speeches by officials seeking to convince young Saudi men that political and social conditions in the country are ideal.

There is, of course, little to support the official government line. Political expression is still constrained, demonstrations remain illegal, and barriers to social mobility continue to be practically insurmountable. But, far from eliminating pluralism and dissent, the authorities have merely driven a community of alienated and embittered Saudis underground and onto the Internet, where hundreds of websites have emerged, the most extreme preaching the ideas of al-Qaida and its ideological ilk.

## Confrontation and violence

Spurred on by unemployment, political uncertainty, and falling living standards, young Saudi men are easy recruits to Osama Bin Laden's creed, prepared to die for their heavenly reward. After all, the rulers' attempt at theocratic validation has not eliminated public accountability.

On the contrary, in the eyes of a people inculcated with Islamic teachings, the rulers' use of religious dogma as the basis of political legitimacy merely exposes them to a standard of rule and behaviour that they do not – indeed *cannot* – meet.

The rise in extremist violence in recent years reflects the slow pace of reform that inevitably results from the rulers' continued reliance on Islam as an ideological crutch. Since May 2003 Saudi Arabia has become a central theatre for terrorist operations, including attacks on the US consulate in Jeddah, the Ministry of Interior, the police headquarters in Riyadh, and the industrial facilities in Yanbu. For people despairing of the prospects of reform and real public participation, the mode of action has become one of direct confrontation with the state.

The young Saudi population, in particular, is at a crossroads, with pragmatists, liberals, and moderates on one side, and radical Salafis on the other. But, while the state should not be afraid of the moderates, it represses, censors, silences, and even imprisons them, while appeasing the religious radicals. To be sure, the authorities have killed some of the more violent jihadis in their 'war on terror', but only a few in relative terms, owing to fear of upsetting the extremists' strong tribal base.

## The endless dilemma

High oil prices in the past two years have brought little change to ordinary peoples lives, owing to rampant corruption and the voracious spending habits of the 22,000 princes and princesses. As in the past, the latest oil windfall has not translated into infrastructure development. What is different now, however, is the continued spread of information technologies that allow frustrated Saudis to discuss the lifestyles of the princes, thereby highlighting the gap between the rich and the poor.

Meanwhile, reforms that would have a sustained effect on security – such as freedom of expression and assembly, competitive elections, recognition of minority rights, modernisation of the education system, and even establishment of social amenities like cinemas and youth clubs – are ignored in the name of defending the state and the faith. The regime's new focus on the domestic 'war on terror' has been used to justify inertia, thus reinforcing the old forms of social exclusion.

In these circumstances, promises of partial elections are too little and too late. With most people unable to see themselves benefitting from, or properly represented in these elections, change is no longer likely to arrive with a ballot box. Instead, reactions range from cynical apathy to frustration, despair, and violence.

Following King Fahd's death in August 2005, despite an apparently smooth succession to his half brother, Abdullah, Saudi Arabia remains a kingdom without a king. During the last ten years of the incapacitated Fahd's rule, divisions between the old, powerful princes widened, and no one knows who has ultimate authority. The princes appear united in fighting terrorism, yet they are incapable of agreeing on matters of reform and democracy. Their dilemma results from a fundamental problem: the absence of a strategy for renewing the legitimacy of their regime. Until the question mark hanging over the monarchy and the place of religion in the political system is removed, the gap between promises of political participation and the reality of popular accountability cannot be bridged.

# American and Western political initiatives in the Middle East

## 8

*Challenges of democratisation in the Middle East
– Case study of Saudi Arabia*

FOWZIYAH ABU-KHALID

*In the Name of Allah, Most Gracious, Most Merciful*

## An opening question

The American sociologist C. Wright Mills once said, "We sometimes fail to understand the nature and the scope of political dilemmas, not because of insufficient information, but because of lack of imagination". This means that the importance is not to give more information than that generously offered by the media and the Internet every second of the day, but to fuel and trigger the imagination of the situation and to envision different alternatives for both peace and democracy in the Middle East and worldwide.

When the Americans, for instance, invaded Iraq, they expected their troops to be received with flowers after weeks of continuous bombing of civilian targets. Such a false expectation was not the result of lack of information, but of imagination and vision of an objective reality beyond the American dream of expansion. It was built on the American illusionary self-image as a representative of the free and "democratic" world.

Thus, the opening question of this paper is this: Are we ready to allow ourselves freedom of imagination in order to develop a new vision for international relations and for the Middle East outside the boundaries of the stereotyped version?

## An opening statement

The reality experienced daily by Arabs and Muslims in various forms is that the major internal/external challenge for democratisation in the Arab world is the conflict with Israel. This is a necessary beginning when dealing with democratisation in Saudi Arabia or any other parts of the Arab region. This is simply – but inevitably – so because the Palestinian issue is a key question for reaching an objective understanding of the region. It represents a personal as well as a national importance for most Arabs in order for any one of them to be engaged in a productive dialogue. Without realising and acknowledging the real meaning of the continuous unjust situation of the Palestinian people, it would be a mere illusion to seek a constructive relationship between the West and the Arab world. In addition, there is the question of the American occupation of Iraq, which today introduces another internal/external complexity to the scene and to the challenges of democracy in the region.

## An Arab public opinion on Western initiatives for democratisation of the Middle East

The first and most famous initiative put forth by the US and the West, towards solving the conflicts in the region. was the American initiative, called "The Broader Middle East and North Africa Initiative". However, this initiative was met with suspicion in the Arab world, regarding the American agendas for the region; especially that it was launched at the same time as the US missiles against civilians in Afghanistan and Iraq.

Therefore, in this paper we cannot ignore the question whether the aim of this American initiative is to help reform the region, or to impose a reality that makes the US presence in the area acceptable, while trying unsuccessfully to disguise its occupation by using the long lost dream of democracy and the chronic oppression of freedoms in the Arab world.

Denmark has also presented its own plan for the Middle East from Morocco to Iran. This initiative for democratic reforms submitted by the Danish government to the international community and to the Arab world in the summer of 2003, with a time table stretching from 2005 to 2009, is important on its own, and yet it cannot be separated from other European efforts to emulate American hegemony in the world.

Consequently, we must stop and ask some questions regarding these Western initiatives of political reform, before they are either accepted or rejected by the official Arab leaderships in the region, without giving a say to the intellectuals and the Arab public. Some of these questions are:

1) What is the real objective behind these American and European initiatives, and can they all be grouped together?
2) What is the political aim of the initiatives with regard to the relationship between the Arab world and the countries that originate them?
3) What is the intellectual framework of the initiatives?
4) Do they take into consideration the realities and needs faced by the societies they approach, and the nature of the social powers in the Arab world?
5) Are they introduced on the basis of equal international relations, or of a dominant relationship with the region, its history, culture, dreams, needs, and values, assuming that what benefits Western societies should benefit Arabs?
6) Do they make it a priority to reform the region and stabilise it, or to serve the needs of the issuers of these initiatives, and their own interests, such as Israel?
7) Are they based on recognising the rights of different nations to develop their own democratic alternatives or patterns, or do they represent one single alternative with a coercive means of imposing it?
8) Could these initiatives be a tool to bring together societies and common issues in an international community that desperately needs to rethink the current power balance which is based on dominance and hegemony?
9) How objective can the initiatives be, not only with respect to relations with others, but also with themselves? In other words, is their a vision of the region and its people free of European or American centrism?

10) What democratic credibility do these initiatives have with regards to Guantanamo, Abu-Ghraib, and the Palestinian people under Israeli occupation? Can they acknowledge the democratic breakdown that these grave incidents represent? What of the recent pressure from the US on the UN not to support the Third Arab Human Development Report after it dared to criticise US policies in Iraq? Not to mention the Neo-conservatives' dominance of US politics, imposing their ideals with regards to the international community. Here we must ask, doesn't the re-election of G.W. Bush to a second term, despite all the internal failures his first term in office recorded in terms of Americans' rights and needs, as well as the disaster of war and occupation of Iraq, represent a breakdown in US democracy?

Although some of these initiatives bring back memories of Europe's division of Arab lands under the Ottoman Empire rule early last century, in the name of saving them from oppression and helping Arabs to establish a great unified and independent Arab nation in 1916, we still point out some considerable differences between American initiatives and those offered by Europe.

The most important difference is that they don't stem from similar policies towards the region, neither in the case of their presence in it nor the nature of their relationship with its countries and societies. However, a major similarity between the American and European initiatives is their objective to try to resolve the instability of the region. It should be pointed out that this instability is a result of factors caused by the historical relationship of the West with the region's struggles starting with Balfour's promise to allocate Palestinian land for the occupation and settlement of Israel, and not ending with the US policies of backing a number of undemocratic regimes in the region.

Despite the fact that in the Arab world the leadership's policy towards these initiatives is usually sufficient, there is a noticeable move at least in the media to open up channels of discussion about the initiatives, especially that they are concerned with reforms which no government or single leader can solve alone, in a time when outside threats are targeted at both the rulers and the ruled of the Arab world.

Therefore, the welcoming of these initiatives in the Arab world is a wary one – even from liberal factions, because there is a general feeling in the region that although international relations are welcome they shouldn't be based on blind obedience. There is also a general feeling in the Arab and Islamic world of a need to initiate one's own internal reforms away from outside influence. Furthermore, some social powers in the Arab world are trying to face the new situation caused by official policies towards democratic reform, since many Arab governments see implementing this reform as simply forming committees to satisfy the US and the West, and to cover up their political dominance, without actually carrying out any of these reforms.

Taking into consideration the above argument and questions of the Arab public opinion towards American and Western political initiatives in the Middle East may help to develop a more constructive image of internal/external challenges of democracy and reform in the Arab world in general and in Saudi Arabia in particular.

## Saudi Arabia and political reforms

Within the framework of the given political structure in Saudi Arabia and the existing relations of power, one can talk about a number of contesting elements that are facing the demands for political reforms in Saudi Arabia today. The main internal dilemmas that face democratisation in Saudi Arabia today can be specified in the following way:

1) The first challenge facing reform in Saudi Arabia is the very political structure of Saudicity and the internal logic of the political discourse of Saudism, which imprison the Saudi leadership today in their traditional mode of power relations. Therefore, despite the internal and external pressure to replace the exclusive mode of power relations with a democratic mode of political participation that would include different social forces of the Saudi society, the Saudi officials are still reluctant to actualise their daily announcement of their intention of political reforms.

2) The second challenge is the long absence of freedom of speech and difference of opinion in Saudi Arabia. Despite the latest relative

loosening of the traditional strict measures on public opinion, there is still a long way to go for both the government and the society to establish a democratic measure for freedom of speech and expression.

3) The denial of multiplicity in the society. Realising the historical multiplicity of the Saudi society geographically and culturally and the growing diversity of new social forces shows how denial of this diversity poses a serious challenge for reform.

4) The invisibility of women on the public scene, which allows for exclusion of half the society from political participation. Although a number of steps have been taken by the Saudi officials towards rethinking the women's question in the Saudi society, especially under the growing pressure of highly educated women, all that has been offered on a practical scale shows a considerable amount of hesitation to allow women the fully-fledged rights of citizenship. As an example of these steps taken to grant women some of their social and political rights as Muslims and Saudi nationals, the Third National Dialogue conference was held in Al- Madina Al-monoarah 2004 to discuss the issue. Official invitations were sent from the organisers of the conference to a group of over 100 men and women from different socio-political backgrounds and from different regions in the Kingdom to participate in this dialogue. Since I was one of the participants I had the chance to see firsthand the positive effects of the dialogue, although most of the final recommendations regarding women's political rights have not yet been implemented. The positive points are as follows:

a. The coming together of women from all intellectual and academic levels and schools of thought, from liberals to fundamentalists, and for the first time in Saudi political history, the ability of these women to recognise their differences and the possibility of dialogue to reach a common ground and social benefits.

b. The reception by Crown Prince Abdullah bin Abdul Aziz of the women participants in his *"majlis"* in the presence of his wife and his listening to their requests for reform with regards to women in society, including women's political rights. This was one of the rare times that direct contact between a group of Saudi women and one of the main decision-makers in the Saudi government was made.

c. The reception of a group of women from the conference by members of the High Commission for Religious Scholars, and the discussion between them of issues pertaining to women's social rights, including the right to drive.

5) The fifth challenge is the absence of a written legal and Shari'a system that legalises political activities.

6) There is political neutralisation if not marginalisation of non-governmental actors and civil institutions. Up until this moment and despite the government's initiative of forming official committees for human rights and the like, the government is still reluctant to give permission to the public to form independent civil committees in that direction.

7) There is the social fear of Westernisation and cultural erosion which makes the Saudis very cautious of both liberal and Western approaches. Sometimes these two approaches are not differentiated from each other because of the fear of losing cultural identity for some people and of losing power privileges for others.

Nevertheless, there has recently been a number of political initiatives introduced on the road to reforms, such as Crown Prince Abdullah bin Abdul Aziz's initiative of establishing a centre for "National Dialogue", the recent move for municipal elections (although excluding women), and increasing the number of members in the Shura Council (although they also excluded women, and are still based on a system of appointment and not elections).

However, some of these initiatives are either too late or too little, or both. They are also becoming a source of growing dispute and disagreement. In addition, there is the fact that public initiatives are not encouraged (e.g. the elite's petitions for political reform led to the confiscation of a number of their leaders).

# 128

## Conclusion

Since Sep. 11th, 2001, Saudi Arabia has been going through internal and external pressures to give up its old tribal mode of power relations and allow the development of fully-fledged civil institutions and the participation of different social forces in the decision making. In other words, there is an urgent need now for a complete political reform and not only for improvement or development of some social services. There is also a need for political recognition of different social forces including women, and for involving them in the processes of facing internal and external challenges to establish democratic reforms and to strengthen national solidarity.

To develop a sense of an alternative initiative to those introduced by the Americans and/or the West, I end this paper by highlighting the main suggestions and recommendations for political reforms in Saudi Arabia, which were initiated by a number of Saudi activists and academics from different parts of the country, and from various socio-political backgrounds. We introduced these suggestions and recommendations as they were written in a petition presented to Crown Prince Abdullah bin Abdul Aziz on the 22nd of Dhul Qi'da, 1424 AH (2003) signed by a few hundred Saudi citizens.

## Suggestions and recommendations for political reforms in Saudi Arabia

1) Accelerating political reform
2) Increasing public involvement
3) Electing the Shura Council and regional boards
4) Establishing syndicates and civil associations and organisations
5) Developing communication channels between the government and its citizens
6) Controlling the economy in order to safeguard public wealth
7) Consolidating the culture of open discussion and tolerance and fighting extremism
8) Developing academic curricula and expanding scientific knowledge
9) Guaranteeing freedom of thought and expression

10) Reinforcing the role of women in society
11) Liberating youth from the dominance of extremism and extravagance
12) Respecting intellectual and sectarian differences

# Democratisation in future Iraq

AMAL SHLASH

Neither the process of democratisation nor that of modernisation can be expected to be carried out unproblematically in a country like Iraq, located as it is in the politically hot area and oil-rich region of the Middle East. Add to that the inhospitable, unnatural and unfavourable external environment that has existed since World War 1.

The importance of establishing democracy in the Middle East has exceeded the internal evolutionary process that pushes the society to express its needs for freedom and human rights. Today, that process emerges largely as a globalisation spill-over and is associated with international efforts to achieve peace and fight terrorism, rather than responding to local expectations and inspirations. However, one cannot deny that favourable changes in the external environment provide a great opportunity and a dynamic ignition to the process of democratisation. But one could ask, if this process could take place smoothly and calmly. There are many reasons unfortunately that point towards a negative answer.

Occupation has made the Iraqis more aware of the necessity to defend and thus reorganise, their own religious and cultural systems. This fact leads to the important recognition of how they face or deal with occupation. It is being debated whether to meet the occupation by rejection, adaptation or integration, but lessons from history show that the return to an "idealized historical or religious form of government has often been seen as a shield against foreign or modern intrusion".[66]

We should also remember that Britain was the only country where modernisation and democratisation were accomplished gradually in relative peace over a period of more than 200 years. In contrast, in France the democratic evolution was marked by violence.

## Democracy and security

However this should not offset the strong will of the Iraqis to go forward with the process. Shortly before the elections a survey about the willingness of the Iraqi people to build democracy in spite of the occupation was conducted by the Iraqi ministry of planning, the UNDP and FAFO (the Norwegian labor union's research institute) with around 3,300 Iraqi people. They were asked a few important questions about their standard of living and about their future aspirations. The survey showed that 75 percent of the sample is very interested in elections, considering it their key to building a new future. Despite the fact that they were 80 percent Arabs, 15 percent Kurds, and 5 percent from other communities – and despite their being Muslims, Christians or from other religions, religion proved not to have any impact or effect on the percentage of responses to the survey.

People also linked the fulfilment of the election result with the security situation, revealing that the priority of the Iraqis is to regain a steady and secure life, which is the most important factor in building democracy, and not the other way round where people see democracy as an approach to achieving security.

This paper will try to explain the factors behind the democratisation deficiency and to provide some broad suggestions on how to overcome existing challenges. The war on Iraq followed by the occupation has in fact exposed the deep and multi-dimensional economic, social, political and cultural crisis of this country which has been inherited from the

---

66  Ahmedou Ould- Abdallah, UN special representative for West Africa, foreword to *Modernization and Democratization in the Muslim World*, by Shireen T. Hunter, CSIS April 2004.

past and to which many people, including historians and sociologists, attribute the country's deficiency in modernisation and democratisation. In this paper I will particularly look at the economic side of the challenges and obstacles to democratisation of Iraq.

## Challenges

### Strong dependence on oil

After more than five decades of efforts to modernise Iraq, the country still lags not only behind the advanced Western countries but almost every country in the region and the developing countries, except the least developed poor countries. This is so in spite of the fact that Iraq used to be one of the richest middle-income countries in the region in the 1970s because of its natural resources. Iraq is also distinguished by a great balance between its area, its population and its natural resources, and in addition Iraq owns the world's second largest oil reserves. The oil sector dominates Iraq's economy, currently constituting 74 percent of its GDP, and the country depends entirely on oil export for financing investments and expenditures. Oil exports provide more than 93 percent of government revenues and 98 percent of foreign currency earnings. Consequently, the total budget of the government is completely dependent on oil revenues. Although Americans after the occupation are handling this sector, it finances the budget which was about $18 billion for the year 2004, and is estimated to rise to $23, $31 and $32 billion for the following years until 2007. Also the rationing system of food is totally dependent on oil revenues. The dependence on oil is a major weak point in the Iraqi economy.

### The exclusive role of the state

Another main challenge is the necessity of changing the role of the state in Iraq, because the building of a democracy needs two major changes in the structure of the Iraqi political and economic system. The political one is the transition from national unification to pluralisation of the political system. The economic one is the transition from a centralised planned economy towards market economy. These two challenges are difficult and it will be a long process.

As regards the economic transformation, one should point out the distinctive characteristic of the Iraqi economy, or the Iraqi system, which is the excessive role of the state and the weakness of the private sector. This situation is a consequence of a state-managed economic development during the last half century. Due to the former governments' adaptation of a socialist model for development, and the militarisation of the economy and the society, it is difficult to reform this structure and to privatise and liberalise the economy. The dominance of the state in the economic life of the Iraqi society has pushed the balance of power in favour of the state and against society.

The public sector is over-represented in the economy – a fact that has caused inefficiency. Many small- and medium-sized enterprises have weakened over the last thirty years and due to its extensive weakness the private sector has limited its role in the economic development, increasing the lack of diversification in the economy. It is impossible to start a privatisation process now since Iraq does not have a private sector of small- and medium-sized enterprises that are strong enough to withstand the competition from other foreign investors. Most of the industrial sector, i.e. around 84 percent, is dependent on the public sector administration, despite the fact that privatisation was a priority for the economic reform programme when it started in 2003. Because the Iraqi private sector is extremely weak and – being under socialism for 35 years – a capitalist class is lacking and it will take some time to establish a healthy ground for a national private sector to grow.

### Lack of modernisation[67]

1) Socio-economic indicators explain important challenges to democratisation. Disparities and social inequalities are widespread in a broad range of fields covering health, education, as well as

---

67 For details on the present and future trends of the Iraqi economy see "Iraq's National Development strategy (2005-2007)" ISRB, Ministry of Planning and Development Cooperation, Iraq September 2004.

public and social services for the low income groups, i.e. internally displaced persons, refugees, single parent-households (11 percent) and vulnerable groups across the country. More than 50 percent of the population of Iraq being under 24 years of age, Iraqi youth is nevertheless alienated due to violence and limited access to education, training and career prospects. Iraq suffers from extensive unemployment – ranging from 40 to 50 percent – and deep poverty among more than 28 percent of the population in some areas of Iraq, despite the fact that the oil-for-food-programme includes the ration-food-basket providing basic needs for the people.

2) The illiteracy rate is high and it is higher among women (41 percent) and schoolchildren expressing gender inequalities, and there is a high level of unemployment especially among the young people (33 percent) and among women.

3) There are highly skewed patterns of income distribution with a small rich minority while the rest of the population is trapped in various degrees of poverty; all of it as a result of a biased allocation of resources and waste of resources because of the militarisation of the economy.

4) There are regional disparities too, some governorates are poor and others are in fact richer but cannot depend on their resources because of the centralised system and centralised resource-allocation in Iraq. As it happens, the richest governorates Basra, Kirkuk and Amara have almost all the oil of Iraq and at the same time they are the poorest governorates in the country.

5) Distorted patterns of urbanisation. The major outcome of such a situation is the absence of citizenship, the phenomena that establishes the rights and duties of each individual in the society and the relation between the citizen and the state. Such an understanding is crucial to Democracy. Like most Arab Countries the rural population in Iraq remains quite high (30 percent). However, rapid urbanisation was the result not of large-scale industrialisation but rather of migration of an impoverished rural population to the cities. As urban centres resemble rural areas in terms of cultural values, attitudes, and educational levels, they cannot be seen as a phenomenon of modernisation; rather they represent the displace-

ment of traditional societies (tribal relations) into urban conglom-
erates. Moreover, the pattern of state intervention and political
rule has created a vertical environment where the upper and lower
circuits become disintegrated on the basis of segregation in income
and access to resources, social capital and public services.

6) Deteriorating infrastructure. Although the whole economy is depending on oil, this sector is in need of a major rehabilitation of
its infrastructure to regain its pre-1991 capacity when it produced
around 3.5 million barrels a day. Some estimates assume that it
will need around $18 billion to increase from 2.5 million barrels
a day – the current capacity – to 3.5 or 3.6. All other areas of
the infrastructure are also suffering, including electricity, water,
telecommunication, transportation, and so on. In the light of this
dangerous and worsening reality reconstruction programmes and
the implementation of economic reforms face major challenges and
there is little progress in executing these programmes; indeed the
whole reconstruction process is facing real delays and is moving
more slowly than expected. Slow economic progress and increased
insecurity have contributed to a state of frustration among the
population which, if continued, could threaten the chances of success not only for those programmes but also for building democracy
in the country.

## A few more challenges. Political and social

The first challenge is of course the occupation itself. Although the occupation has the stated aim of building democracy in Iraq it is in itself
a challenge to democracy. This is due to the Bush administration's
adoption of a very ambitious agenda for the political transformation
of Iraq and the region as a whole. According to their declarations they
wanted "Iraq free of weapons of mass destruction and ties to terrorism
and moreover led by a broadly based representative government hereby
taking the first steps towards democracy. The American agenda also
includes a demand for regime change in Iraq in order to secure stability
in oil rich Saudi Arabia, to create the terms to solve the Arab-Israeli
conflict, and to encourage political reforms throughout the region which

is much in need of change".[68] This means that we are facing a long term mission for the Americans in the region. It is therefore unrealistic to think of ending the occupation in this transitional or provisional period as a precondition to building democracy, bearing in mind the Palestinian experience and other lessons from history. The main challenge to the Iraqis now is how to deal with the dilemma of democracy-building within the current occupation of Iraq!!

It is therefore not surprising that people in Iraq still recall memories and lessons drawn from the British occupation of Iraq 1917-1932, and believe that there are many contextual similarities between Iraq then and now.

During the British era in Iraq which lasted for more than four decades, Iraqis became familiar with their first exercise of democracy-building when, due to the absence of strong governmental institutions, politics were highly personalised during the monarchy era (with the Iraqi kings, Faysal I and II, installed by the British). Both the Crown and the British sought to influence the outcome of parliamentary elections in order to secure positions for their preferred candidates. Moreover, many of those who served in parliament did so out of a desire for personal gain, not out of a commitment to public service. Thus democracy eventually became discredited in the eyes of many Iraqis because of political corruption, British meddling, and the government's failure to respond to their needs. Military coups became the primary means by which governments were changed, setting the stage for the eventual overthrow of the monarchy in 1958.

It is worthwhile remembering that although external and internal forces are pushing towards building democracy, Iraqis in post-Saddam Iraq are likely to view US actions as an external factor pushing for democracy seen through the lens of their country's experience during the British era, ending with frustration and the whole process being discredited. Hence the occupation will create a tension which simultaneously will pose obstacles for the achievement of democracy.

---

68   *U.S. policy in post-Saddam Iraq, lessons from the British Experience*, ed. by Micheal Eisenstadt and Eric Mathewson, The Washington Institute for Near East Policy, 2003, p. 68.

There might be cases that are easier to handle than the Iraqi one but the result of a strong state was always a weak society. And that is what we mean by the priority of the Iraqis to have their civil-society institutions built as soon as possible and as strong as possible to get on the track of democratisation of the country.[69] Of course the social and economic factors which we have already mentioned – the existence of large scale poverty, poor electricity supply, poor health conditions and large income disparity – are in, and of, themselves impeding the building of a civil society and democratisation of the country.

These conditions have made the extremists' ideas including those of the radicals, whoever they are, more attractive. This situation inhibits efforts of democratisation because of the fear that extremists could win within a democratic process and then subvert it by establishing a religious type of organisation. This is a challenge that new politicians and governments and the whole Iraqi people are facing.

Another challenge is gender-inequality inherited from the last twenty years. Since Iraq went through wars with its neighbours, women have been the victims of the economic and social policies that the regime undertook during the wars, and the following 13 years of economic sanctions. This situation is pushing women's interests away from political life and therefore discouraging half the population from participating actively and not only through elections.

Some social indicators show yet another discouraging picture. During the Saddam Hussein period there were no parties, no NGOs, no civil society institutions. A precondition for building democracy is of course the existence of such institutions. Last year, in spite of the occupation and whatever was related to that, we witnessed the establishment of 4,000 Iraqi NGOs, ten percent of whom are women NGOs, which is an encouraging step towards building a civil society. The excessive tendency to establish parties and social or political institutions is a healthy phenomenon in itself and it is needed within this transitional period.

---

69   "Inherent Socio-economic problems precluded the development of a strong middle class". And "Under the Ba'ath regime the structural problems of the past have been magnified, and new problems have been introduced. The middle class has all but disappeared". Ibid. p. 24.

## Suggestions

In order to find a way out of these challenges we can suggest a few ideas. Firstly, major support should be given on all levels inside and outside Iraq to the building of a human capital through education and training, including technical and scientific education, and through the encouragement of a spirit of enquiry inside the educational institutions in order to form a new way of thinking and a free mind. Secondly, the income disparities should be reduced through a process of development geared to job creation. This requires seriously building a new private sector in Iraq encouraging the establishment of private organisations. Thirdly, closing gender gaps will be necessary in trying to solve the development problems and to increase political participation.

These goals are best achieved through a culturally sensitive strategy including progressive reading of Iraqi resources themselves. Encouraging a culture of dialogue, tolerance and accommodation is essential both for democracy and for development, of which the country is desperately in need. This can be achieved through supporting the educational and cultural institutions in the country, and encouraging the development of civil society is particularly important for the consolidation of democracy once it has been established.

Fourthly, after being isolated for the last 25 years, the Iraqi economy needs to be reintegrated into the global economy and it should again be a productive part of the international economy inasfar as it is the second largest oil country in the region after Saudi Arabia.

Those are the steps to be taken or suggestions to be discussed on the internal level. On the international level, Iraq is part of the Middle East which is the hottest region in the world now, so it is possible that the success of the democratisation of Iraq is related to resolving the regional conflict as well as the encouragement of regional economic cooperation which is another very important factor, just as important as the political factor. The processes of creating larger markets and reducing regional conflicts are all related to a regional economic cooperation built on the historical, geographical, and cultural aspects of the Arab region.

## Conclusion

History offers a number of lessons for the first steps toward establishing a functioning democracy:

1) If democracy is to take root, it must be built primarily by Iraqis in response to specific Iraqi conditions and needs.
2) The establishment of democratic structures alone is insufficient to produce democratic processes or outcomes. The Iraqis must also create civil society institutions and strengthen basic freedoms, which are essential preconditions for building democracy. Furthermore, significant efforts must be devoted to preventing corruption by fostering transparency, accountability, and the rule of law.

Every Iraqi, woman or man, old or young, wish that the occupation would end and wish that the American forces – and they say American forces not multinational forces – would leave. But the problem is that without democracy it will be a very long and difficult mission for us to end the occupation. We hope that through building democracy through elections we could bring better politicians to the national assembly, because on the 9th of April 2003 we started in a vacuum as we did not have any political party. So building political parties, or having a political life, or working to establish this political culture within the people is a new experience in itself and a long term process.

The question of how Iraq will get control of its major wealth, oil, is a political question. If we are going to accept American control of oil fields, oil extraction and oil export, we will be unable to control our oil. This problem, like the one of privatisation, has been deferred to be dealt with by the new government which will emerge, after the creation of the constitution. It is not possible for a provisional or a transitional government to deal with this for it is the right of the people to decide how to deal with this problem. We think this will be the major challenge that the new elected government is going to face. After thirty years of a nationalised oil industry it is difficult from a nationalist perspective to think that we should turn it over to the Americans. This would be a great challenge and we expect that every party will put the oil question as a priority in their economic programme, oil and privatisation.

# The democratic dilemmas in Iraq

## 10

HUDA AL-NU'AIMI

The best description of the evolving Iraqi democracy is that it descended like a parachute. It was clear that democracy could not be acquired simply through words or slogans. There are several objective conditions that need to be satisfied, whether relating to the system, the conduct or the programme. They all complement each other, culminating in processes like identifying the options, taking the decisions and assisting the regular transfer of power.

Democracy in general is the mechanism and method of governance, organisation and management, the right to partake in it, the right to disagree, and the acceptance of other people's views. This entails the accumulative effects of adopting pluralism, diversity and transfer of power.

## Ethnic and sectarian divisions

The decision of the occupying power to dismantle the Iraqi state has contributed dramatically to the spreading of chaos and has deprived the country of security and stability. It has also led to an increase in political turmoil which in itself has reflected negatively on the people's understanding of democracy as meaning freedom to steal, exact revenge and tribal vendettas. But most fundamentally it has led to the explosion of cultural, ethnic, and sectarian divisions.

But the problem does not stop there. Basically, it lies in the power-sharing based on fabricated ethnic and sectarian groupings brought about by, and imposed by the occupier in the manner in which the

Ruling Council and the Transitional Government were set up. One cannot but notice that within this process was the physical elimination, the political exile, the arbitrary dismissal and termination of service that extended to all the elites in Iraq.

One should not pass without giving credit to the Iraqis. Despite the tribal system and the clannish vendettas that have been enhanced and encouraged during many decades, the people of Iraq have so far managed to avoid slipping into the sectarian wars which many analysts expected. In doing so the people of Iraq have managed to solidify their unity and express their cultural and social cohesion.

## A fragmented political scene

Along with the new concept of power-sharing on a sectarian basis, new views have evolved among the Iraqis. Broad sectors of the Iraqi society are doubtful and suspicious about the roles of the new politicians who have propagated such expulsion. The democratic promises, which the US assured the Iraqis to implement, fell into the same dilemma as the previous regime that exiled those who disagreed with them.

On the other side of the Iraqi spectrum, resulting from the invasion, a new wave evolved. This presented itself as political Islam, both Sunni and Shi'a, at a stage where the religious mullahs entered politics, government and elections, in which each took the side of his or her sect and religious affiliation. Even inside the same sect there appeared differences in the methods and the ways of dealing with the occupation. It would not be an exaggeration to say that the religious parties constitute only a small percentage of the Iraqi public. The majority spreads over several organisations with nationalistic, leftist and social affiliation away from sectarian identity.

The fragmentation inside the political parties constitutes a dangerous outcome for democracy in Iraq. Following the occupation, some 232 parties and movements were born. Very few of them have any historical roots in Iraq or popular followings. Most of the new parties were born or created outside Iraq for an imported democracy. It is because of that fragmentation and party division that one sees the weakness of the political programmes being suggested and the difficulty in recognising the legitimacy of diversity, lacking the capacity to manage it. During the election over 200 lists were set up, whereas in fact it would have been possible to reduce that number to a mere 10 lists because of the similarity or identity of most of the programmes. The problem with the Iraqi political parties was not simply the difficulty to come to power but went beyond that, in that many of these parties personalised their lists and relied on religious symbols to propagate their election campaign. The short period given for the campaign and the lack of stability and security contributed to the public ignorance of the candidates' programmes – assuming that the candidates had such programmes! This in turn led to flourishing individualism in Iraqi politics.

The political conduct of Arab regimes towards Iraq following the Kuwait conflict in 1990 and the follow-up of physical and psychological punishment imposed on the people of Iraq under the guise of so-called 'international legitimacy' – all led to a sudden rise of anti-Arabism, to demands that relations with Arab nationalism be severed, and to calls for Iraq to act not as part of the Arab nations but rather as an amalgamation of different groups of Sunnis, Shi'as and Kurds. It even went to the extent that wiping out Iraq's Arab face had become a democratic necessity for all these constituents to coexist in peace.

Despite the campaign for selling democracy, it transpired that political parties intended to come to power as an objective and not a means to invigorate political activity and create a political class. We witnessed a panting rush towards power at any cost. Attaining power became the ultimate objective through militias carrying out assassinations and silencing of dissenters practiced by one party or another. The system gave birth to a new nepotism. The common saying prevailing today is that one Pharaoh has gone only to be replaced by another.

## Presidential or parliamentary system?

The occupying power enacted the Transitional Government Law, thereby giving birth to a new model for government which is both illegitimate and difficult to manage. The executive power consists of a Presidential Council (a President with two deputies) and the National Assembly consisting of 275 members which elects the Presidential

Council by a two-thirds majority. The Presidential Council takes its decisions unanimously, which means that any of its members has the right of veto against any decision or legislation made by the National Assembly. One question that imposes itself here is whether Iraq could adapt to a presidential or parliamentary system: where does the decision-making lie, and what happens when the members of the Presidential Council differ? Article 3 of the Transitional Government Law grants an unelected body, namely the Ruling Council, the authority to bind the National Assembly, which is an elected body, with a law which the Assembly cannot amend with less than three-quarters of its members and the unanimous approval of the Presidential Council. This means that any amendment becomes subject to full agreement and not to the will of the people who are supposed to be the source of power.

Article 49 calling for the deba'athification is contrary to Article 12, which states that all Iraqis are equal before the law and equal in rights and duties irrespective of race, opinion, belief, nationality or religion. Another serious outcome of the Transitional Government Law appears in Article 61 which allows for the adoption of the new constitution through referendum. Such a referendum would be considered successful when the majority of the people vote for it, on the condition that it is not rejected by two thirds of the voters in any three governates. This article is clearly contrary to the principles of democracy which make the will of the people supreme and do not accept the constitution to be dependent on a veto exercised by voters in a few governates.

## Slogans of democracy

The US slogan of democratising political life in Iraq does not carry any believable weight due to the scale of violence by the occupying power and its persistence in imposing many unfair policies that have so far antagonised the public and caused eruption of anger in many parts of the country. Some of these policies have been exercised with such a violence and brutality that the Iraqis are convinced that they have no human value and that the Americans can do whatever they like with them. These policies and practices are increasingly similar to what has been happening in Palestine at the hands of the Israeli occupying authority in the form of the killing of civilians, destruction of houses, scorching land, erecting concrete walls and making arbitrary arrests.

## Women and human rights

History records that Iraqi women have played a role in several fields in Iraq since the beginning of the Iraqi state. It is no coincidence that Iraq was the vanguard of women's uprising in the Arab world. The first Arab woman to be a minister was Naziiha Ad-Dulaimi during the rule of General Qasim after the 1958 coup. Women's efforts have achieved a good deal of freedom and liberation through the promulgation of the Family Law No. 188 of 1959.

Despite the progressiveness of many valid laws regarding women, their influence was, however, limited because of old tribal customs and traditions. More important, women's efforts enabled the country to go on with the economic and daily life during the 1980s when Iraqi men were fighting in the Iran-Iraq war. Since then the Iraqi women's role in the daily life has become a burden, limiting their contribution in many official and practical sectors.

Years of sanctions against Iraq have had their political, economic, social and technical consequences which affected both men and women and imposed extra stress on women, particularly in having to accommodate both domestic and work responsibilities. However, through that experience Iraqi women acquired the capacity and competence to carry out various kind of jobs in the official as well as private sectors.

After the occupation of Iraq, women became aware of the fact that their role and position in society should ascend to new activities in forming policies and making decisions and to contribute to the process of development and reconstruction. However, the intensity of discrimination against women and the increase in women's worries about their rights after the Law Number 173, issued by the Transitional Governing Council, which was later repealed through a US order, has signalled the start of a new era of marginalisation and denial of women's rights. The Iraqi society may have started entrenching itself into parties and groups and has become more polarised by its change to a multi-party system.

It is unrealistic to assume that party activity has become cleansed of old beliefs and concepts regarding woman and her role in society and family. Domination over women is an obvious symptom that burdens women in Iraq. The domination by father, husband or brother shows in punishment, limitation of freedom, fear of dialogue and expression, false respect and total obedience. The fear that the women could fall into disgrace has become the guideline that controls a woman's behaviour. Obedience to the man is the basis of her decisions and determination of her destiny. Her allegiance to family and tribe has taken over her sense of identity and allegiance to the nation.

The Constitution must bestow legitimacy on women's rights and form the basis of protection for those rights. It should also bind everybody to respect them, because a woman is a human being entitled to these basic rights and freedoms. In addition to what the Constitution can contribute, there is a need for a modification of the cultural, social and behavioural styles of both men and women through a civilised, educational and cultural process supported by legislation.

It is possible that human rights as a guarantee to protect man's right to enjoy a decent life in general be based on two principles. Firstly human dignity is identified in the Holy Quran in its saying: "We have dignified the sons of Adam". We also have to remind ourselves of the international conventions regarding human rights. The International Declaration on Human Rights states in its preamble that the human dignity enshrined in the human society is the basis of justice and peace, emphasised in Article 1 on human dignity.

Secondly, total equality for all people. Basic human rights and freedom reject discrimination whatever its cause or source. All people are equal in rights and obligations despite the diversity of their culture, colour or race. This natural distinction should not in any way be the cause of discrimination among them with regard to their entitlement to enjoy their basic rights and freedoms. The third article of the second chapter of the International Covenant on civil and political rights stipulates that all parties undertake to ensure equality between men and women in their ability to enjoy all civil and political rights stated in the covenant. Within the general principles of human rights some parts of society are granted extra protection and guarantees through international conventions and legislations, such as the rights of woman and child with special needs. In other words, this kind of specialisation intends to set up new local and international dimensions that aim to show them consideration.

The main principle in demanding human rights for women may be summarised in ensuring the application of equality between men and women in enjoying the same rights whether they be political, civil, economic, educational or cultural, and in ensuring the practical application of these rights in reality.

In order to ensure equality between men and women, the constitution must adopt the principle of rejecting discrimination in rights and obligations. All laws relating to women issues in accordance with the Constitution draw their jurisdiction from this principle, which leads to the natural rejection of any action contradicting this principle.

## Political rights

Based on the above, the women's political rights may be categorised as:

1) The right to vote in all elections,
2) The right to be nominated in all elections,
3) The right to join any political party,
4) The right to partake in formulating policies and their implementation,
5) The right to take any official position in government,
6) The right to join and act in any NGO,
7) The right to represent the state on international level,
8) The right to join international organisations.

We are thus obliged to concentrate our efforts to awaken men in order to change their mentality and attitudes towards women. The problem does not lie in allowing a woman to enter her name on an election list or to encourage some women to take up leading positions or seats in legislative bodies. It lies in the mutual conviction between men and women of the necessity of joint action. Still there is a fear of change of mind among men regarding constitutional legislation in favour of women, arising out of the prevailing vision of domination of women in her conventional role as a housewife.

## Civil rights

The woman has the right to sue, prosecute, grant and receive power of attorney. She has the right to inherit, make a will and assume guardianship if she is an adult. Legislation must take into account the adherence to basic human rights in case a person is charged under criminal law. These legislations should acknowledge that a person is innocent until proven guilty and provide him with proper defence. A person should not be arrested without a warrant issued by an investigating magistrate following an act deemed illegal by the law. The basic legislation should ensure that anyone arrested must be brought before a competent court within the shortest period of time. The law should ensure that a house ought not to be searched unless such an order is made by a magistrate and such search is conducted in the presence of two witnesses and the district elected mayor.

International Human Rights law bans torture, making it a crime against humanity which is punishable by imprisonment. This is important to emphasise in order to form a democratic system that guarantees human beings, men or women, their basic human dignity and rights. After the occupation, women when arrested for no reason had mostly been apprehended on the word of an informer. They felt that power worked as the only legitimacy. Women have also been taken hostages in order to get a son, a father or a husband, wanted by the occupying power, to give himself up. It is regrettable that such measures are still practiced, casting doubt on the democratic system even before its birth.

## Economic rights

Economic rights include the right of the woman to own property in her own right separately from her husband, father or brother and her right to dispose of such property in any form she chooses. She should be allowed to enjoy the wealth of the nation equally with men and to freely work in trading and financial sectors.

## Educational rights

A woman should be entitled to full education up to higher education and should be allowed to receive scholarships to study abroad. This right should be equal to both genders. Intensive campaigns should be undertaken to teach the elderly who have dropped out of the system during the years of sanctions after Iraq eradicated illiteracy during the 1970s and 1980s.

## Social rights

Women make up almost half of each society and give birth to the other half. They should be able to live with full entitlement and rights. Her person and privacy must be protected. She should be free to marry whoever she chooses without any compulsion and should be free to seek divorce or separation while at the same time enjoying the right of custody of her children. Society must offer her and her children proper social care. Women are entitled to criminalise physical assault and violence to which women are subjected, in accordance with the international convention banning all sorts of discrimination against women as approved by the United Nations on December 18, 1979.

In order to ensure the contribution of women in the development process, a democratic environment is required which encourages free expression on an equal basis according to rights and obligations and under the supervision of official constitutional and legal institutions and under the complete independence of the three centres of power, namely the legislative, the judicial and the executive.

We are thus in need of a proper political administration that ensures the genuine role of the woman as an effective force in society. Such an administration should exceed the concepts of women's role that originate from social, cultural and religious concepts.

Despite all this, women also have to learn that rights are not granted but must be obtained. Women should not expect to celebrate victory, they should expect a long-term struggle and endurance in order to rehabilitate society and eliminate many of the inherited historical legacies. There seems to be quite a way between a written constitution and a reality motivated by the concepts of the past.

We are aware of the difficulty of the Iraqi position because of the lack of security and peace and the prevalence of tribal affiliation that enables the latter to enjoy absolute priority at the expense of allegiance to nation and state. We should be aware of the political manifesto that emphasises the role of women, while at the same time watch out for those who at present and in the future – in real life – would like to restrict her role.

The question is what the state should do with regard to women. It is necessary that the state plays an important role through:

1) Formulating a national policy to improve the conditions for women in general in which a specialised group of both genders take part,
2) Enhancing public awareness that adopts nationalism and rejects sectarianism and defends human values and rights,
3) Spreading democratic culture and respect for the opinions of others right from the early stages of education; informing people of international conventions especially regarding women and children,
4) Informing women of their legal rights and the way to secure them,
5) Displaying a public media campaign to support the rights of women and shedding light on their various roles and contributions,
6) Maintaining cooperation between Iraqi women's organisations and their counterparts in the Arab and international world in order to exchange advice and appreciate other experiences,
7) The founding and activating of networks of support service for each woman throughout her life.

# Islamophobia in Europe and its impact on the push for democratisation in the Arab world

## 11

JØRGEN S. NIELSEN

## The Hizb l-Tahriri in Amman 1995

Back in the summer of 1995 I spent three months on study leave in Amman and was hanging out with various Islamist groups, e.g. the Islamic Action Front. I also attended a weekly seminar at one of their little centres up in the hills, and in the end I was asked to present a paper myself on the situation of Muslims in Western Europe. I talked in particular about young people and what is happening with the children and grandchildren of immigrants who become acculturated in the West. After the lecture a member of the audience, whom I could identify from previous meetings, where his interventions had indicated that he was a Hizb al-Tahriri, stated very perceptively that young Muslims in the Middle East are in a confrontation with Western-led modernity across a broad front, but young Muslims in Europe are faced with this confrontation on a much broader and deeper level than the people of the Middle East.

## What can we learn from the young Muslims in Europe?

There is little doubt that what happens as regards Muslim communities in Europe has and will have an impact on their countries of origin and, more broadly, on the wider Muslim world. The question is what kind of impact, and how such impact might be transmitted. There are obvious economic impacts. For a long time Turkish development plans included the remittances of migrants as a substantial element. Recently there were references to Moroccan workers remitting billions of Euros back to Morocco. Less noticed has been the upward pressure on property prices in the villages and small-town suburbs to which émigrés send their money. Or I could refer you to the motorway rest place, the *istiraha*, constructed and maintained to Swedish standards, on the main road from Homs to the Abboudiyeh border crossing into Lebanon: putting upward pressure on other *istirahas* in the region.

But are there impacts of a deeper and more substantial nature, impacts which may contribute to the kind of changes in political culture which this conference is about? I have been asked to focus on Islamophobia, and I can see why. But I am reluctant to see this in isolation, so before discussing the topic specifically, I think I need to lay two bits of foundation. First of all what is Islam in Europe? And secondly what is Islamophobia?

## Islam in Europe

Islam in Europe has two spheres. There are the eastern European Muslim places like the Balkans and large parts of Russia. I have a lot of personal connections with Bulgaria and I am very aware of what is going on there. In those places you are talking about Muslim communities who have been long settled, and by long settlement I mean hundreds of years. They are as indigenous as one can possibly be; communities to whom the distinction between, as the Dutch and the French say, autochtone and non-autochtone simply does not apply. Then there is the Muslim community in Western Europe coming out of a very different historical background, namely immigrations into Europe along the routes of the old imperial relations between Europe and its colonies.

These Muslim immigrants arrived and settled in the 1960s and the 1970s, shifting from being immigrant migrant workers to becoming settled families following the immigration stops in 1962 in Britain and in 1973/74 in the rest of Western Europe. During the 1980s there was a change in generations, leading in Britain in 1989 to the Rushdie affair, when Muslims campaigned for the banning of Salman Rushdie's book *The Satanic Verses*, and a few months later in France the first headscarf affair, when a secondary school in a Paris suburb banned a group of Muslim girls from wearing *hijab*. Arguably these two affairs were the first symptoms of a new generation coming to adulthood. Kids were coming out of school and college going into the labour market with expectations. Because of the open access to citizenship, especially in Britain and France, the young immigrants had expectations of social, economic and political participation. But they found themselves being discriminated against, excluded and so on, and we all know what disappointed expectations can trigger. If it had not been Rushdie it would have been something else. Since then, during the 90s, we have seen young Muslims, children and grandchildren of immigrants, becoming increasingly active claiming a place in the public space.

During the 1990s there was growing public concern, which was later triggered by the increasing demand for public visibility by the Muslims themselves. The response from society, from the political elites and from the media was a concern about refugees and asylum seekers, and a new discourse was established. As the 1990s went on this discourse of fear of refugees and asylum seekers was increasingly overlapped with a discourse about Muslims. This was not only an internal European matter, it was a geopolitical matter. The Soviet empire had collapsed 1989/1991, and immediately after that we began to hear talk of Islam as the 'new enemy'.

That talk was quite clearly encouraged by the North American defence industry. President Eisenhower was very wise when he retired and on the way out warned of the dangers of the might of the military industrial complex. And the military industrial complex was quite clearly pushing a discourse of Islam as a 'new enemy' even before Huntington. And then we went through the triumphalism of Francis Fukuyama's end of history to the chaos of Samuel Huntington's clash of civilisations. This was apparently confirmed, but only apparently, by events in Bosnia, Kosovo, Chechnya, the 1st and 2nd intifadas, all leading to the new right targeting Muslims. It is interesting how the French "Front National" shifted its aim from the old secular race discourse, anti-Algerian, and the old anti-Semitic discourse against Jews to increasingly targeting Muslims. Also the British National Party is characterised by that. I'll refrain from commenting on the domestic Danish politics.

All of this becomes focused by 9/11. But the focuses are selective and distorted. On the one hand there is the first obvious focus on security concerns which is very difficult to dismiss as completely imaginary, although I suspect a lot of it is imaginary. There was a fantastic series on BBC2 called "The Power of Nightmares", where they argue that where politicians in the past could sell themselves with visions they now sell themselves with responses to fear, i.e. protecting people against the imaginary dangers outside. The second part of that equation is policies of integration and policies of social inclusion. The two elements are clearly contrasted in the policies of the British government for example: very strong policies of social inclusion and integration but at the same time probably, next to France, the most aggressive policies on security.

On the other hand you also have contrasts between internal and external policy positions where, strangely enough, France and Britain are mirror images of each other. France is seemingly taking domestic policy decisions which are targeted against Muslims, symbolised in the banning of the headscarves in school. Whereas in foreign policy France appears more favourably inclined to the other side of the Mediterranean, Iraq being the obvious case. In Britain, however, domestic policy is very open and inclusive of Muslims and other religious and ethnic groups, whereas the foreign policy seems to be targeted differently, certainly on Iraq. And then in the longer term there is this underlying, simmering issue going right across Europe about Turkey's membership of the European Union. Increasingly it is a discussion which is focused around Turkey's Islamic identity and Europe's alleged Christian identity.

## Islamophobia

The word first appeared in 1989-1990, and our research suggests that it appeared out of a particular local political discussion in a part of London at that time. It was then adopted into American foreign policy discussions in about 1991.

What does Islamophobia signify? Literally it means fear of Islam, but this is strongly criticised by the British scholar Fred Halliday. He insists that we should rather talk about 'Muslim-phobia', a word that does not trip off the tongue as easily as Islamophobia, but Halliday argues that it is not Islam but Muslims that are feared. I am not sure you can make that distinction; it is a bit too fine for my liking. The Islamophobia discourse obviously is being encouraged by the post-Soviet 'Islam new enemy' discourse which again is being encouraged by the defence industry, as I suggested. The public profile of the concept was seriously heightened, and many people think it first appeared, with the Runnymede Trust report on Islamophobia in Britain,[70] published in 1997. And a few years later it was of course exacerbated by responses to 9/11. Together with a fellow researcher I did a report for the European Monitoring Centre on Racism and Xenophobia[71] in which Denmark got some pretty sharp comments.

The problem with Islamophobia is that it tends to allow an easy categorisation of events and issues into blocks. Particular points of view, analyses, and political positions can be dismissed as islamophobic. The discourse of Islamophobia tends to block constructive discussions and block constructive policy development and responses. Interestingly, some Muslim leaders in Europe seriously object to the whole concept of Islamophobia. They fear that it is too similar to the whole discourse of anti-Semitism and fear that it will push Muslims into a permanent state of victimhood, taking away from them the space to take their own initiatives, to have a degree of control over their own place and development in European life.

Chris Allen with whom I did the above report is just finishing his doctorate on this subject, and he is discovering that there are certain parts of the anti-Semitism lobby in Britain which have encouraged the Islamophobia discourse. There is a suspicion of an alliance being encouraged between the two groups for unclear reasons.

The Western European Muslims' views of them, and their position in Europe, are rather more complex than the Islamophobia discourse. There was in the nineties a widespread suspicion among many young articulate Muslims that what was going on in Bosnia and the delay in Western intervention in Bosnia were deliberate and planned – and was

---

70  Runnymede Trust, *Islamophobia: A challenge for all*, London: Runnymede Trust, 1997.

71  C. Allen and J. S: Nielsen, *Summary Report on Islamophobia in the EU after 11 September 2001*, Vienna: EUMC, 2002; available www.eumc.eu.int.

part of a longer term strategic goal to rid Europe of its Muslims. In other words, they feared they were ultimately next in line. Subsequent events particularly in Kosovo tended to ease that, because the Western intervention was that much smarter and quicker. In Britain, Tony Blair was flavour of the month among Muslim community's leaders during the Kosovo period. But the suspicion is still there, with the French headscarf issue and the absence of response to Chechnya and Palestine which is, still 15 years later, very often contrasted with the rapid Western response to the invasion of Kuwait in 1991. There is the general perception that Muslims in Europe are an underclass, that their interests do not sit very high on the agenda of the politicians and the political elites – although this also is rather more complex.

## Where does this take us?

If you look at the media in the Middle East and more broadly in the Muslim world there is a widespread Muslim and Arab perception of an islamophobic West, and there is actually a widespread tendency to sympathise with the "clash of civilisations" idea. Huntington ironically is now nowhere more popular and more acknowledged than in parts of Arab and Muslim society. There is almost a mirror image between Huntington's "clash of civilisations" idea and political Islamism. We have the irony of endless conferences since '93 when his article first appeared, conferences on the topics of "Clash of civilisation", Islam and the West, Arabs and Europe etc. etc., with the explicit or implicit intention of combating, of deconstructing Huntington's idea. There have been very few conferences on Islam in the West that have taken place with the purpose of confirming Huntington, but by setting up the "Islam" and the "West" discourse in those terms, the participants implicitly confirm Huntington's concept of civilisations as blocks with borders between them. The recent war in Iraq also introduced question marks. There is a very interesting comment by Muhammed Salim Elawa in his weekly column in the Egyptian magazine *Al-Usbu'* just before the war. Here he criticises the statement from the Sheikh Al-Azhar which talked about this war of the West against Islam. Very simply, Muhammed Salim's answer to this was, "look, the Russians are against this, that is the Orthodox; the Germans are against it' that is the Protestants; the French are against it, that is the Catholics, and the largest demonstration against it on the 15th of February 2003 was in London. Where is this Western Christian block?" That reflected the widespread perception in my view among a lot of young Arab intellectuals. I was in Algeria in the week after the beginning of the war and was talking to a lot of younger students who were working part-time as journalists around the conference that I was at, and they all basically agreed with this view and some volunteered it before they had heard about it.

There is a danger that the perception of European Islamophobia strengthens the common and often suspiciously correct idea about the Western double standards. The concept in the Middle East, in the Muslim world, the idea that the West is Islamophobic, is regularly reinforced by the blatant contrast between the "preaching" of Western politicians and their practice. I cannot see how one can see Bush's state of the union message other than as a revivalist evangelical sermon. The same with Blair: in the satirical weekly magazine *Private Eye* there is regularly a column where Blair is made to write his weekly newsletter to his congregation as the vicar of St. Albion's. This preaching is undermined by practice, actual and perceived.

The impact of European Muslim communities and their experience of the Muslim world generally, and their countries of origin particularly, are very complex. It is important to remember that the countries of origin are not just Arab and Turkish they are also South Asia, south East Asia, parts of Africa, Sub Saharan Africa, East and West, basically once you start looking at it, countries of Muslim origin are everywhere in the world. The impact and experience of the Muslim immigrants in Europe on the countries of origin is significant, a lot of it still not measured, recorded, assessed but it is definitely complex. We have past examples: French Algerian involvement in the war of independence up to 1962 was massive. In one year towards the end of the 1950s tens of thousands of French Algerian residents in France were in prison for suspicion of supporting the war of independence on the other side of the Mediterranean. German Turkish involvement in the Turkish civil strife leading up to the coup of September 1980 was massive both on the left and on the right and among the Islamic groups. Pakistani politicians in the period after Zia ul-Haq were recruiting support among Pakistani communities in Britain to the extent that Bhutto's return found a springboard in supporters in the Pakistani communities in Britain. Going outside the Muslim world momentarily, Birmingham was the main external centre of support – some would argue it was the capital of the Sikh independence movement for Khalistan in the 1980s. Incidentally, the Indian deputy high commissioner was assassinated in Birmingham at that time. Nobody talked about Sikh terrorism at the time. Finally we can of course speculate about Europe providing safe houses for al-Qa'ida-type activities.

Less documented is the continuing interaction between immigrant communities and their communities of origin. I currently have a research student who has looked at young Pakistanis in Birmingham returning to their families on short visits, for marriage or otherwise, in parts of Pakistan. The complex transfer and exchange of ideas and perceptions within that community through people moving back and forth is still having an impact which is impossible to assess or measure. The reason is that the images and the perceptions that move with these young people from Birmingham, to Mirpur in Kashmir in particular, change character as they go along. People also have interests in encouraging particular views from their own particular perspectives of the other side that they come from. There is a whole complex of local networks, of family networks, which are extremely active, massive in size, but very difficult to assess in terms of what the impact will be. It will be much easier in thirty years time to come back and research it after the event.

There are two dimensions to the interaction between the immigrant community and the countries of origin. There are the international visitors, like students who return, and the experience that they have while they are in Copenhagen or Birmingham, or wherever, for three or four years is extremely important to the long term perception or image that they go back with. If they have a positive experience here it will gradually build up a different perception there.

As for the loyalty of Muslim and other minority communities within Europe, it is basically the old question of social contract. It is a question of give and take. If they feel that they are being acknowledged, that they have a fair share in the participation, in public life, in the political system, locally and nationally, a fair share of the resources of the country, and that when people talk about poverty, when people talk about education, exclusion etc. it is not just the white working class they are talking about, it is also the brown and the black working class. When a politician calls for a new debate on a new Danish consensus, that debate cannot be won if it is held among white Danes after which the non-white Danes are invited to sign at the bottom. It is a debate which has to include the non-white Danes, otherwise it cannot work. The inclusion will generate loyalty and if there is no inclusion you do not deserve the loyalty.

Related to the migration is the whole business of the interaction of organisations in the countries of origin and the countries of settlement. You might be familiar with the way Muslim organisations, as for example L'Union des Organisations Islamiques en France, the Muslim Brotherhood organisation in France, is described by the press. The same goes for the Islamic Foundation in England, that is regarded as the Jamiati Islami organisation in Britain. The press does not take into consideration the fact that these organisations have changed significantly in terms of their agendas, in terms of the ways they work and in terms of their views, Islamic theological views, as well as their practical programmes. If the founder of Jamiati Islami, Abu Ala Mawdudi who died in 1997, saw what was going on in the Islamic foundation in Britain now he would very likely be horrified.

Finally, and in some ways most dangerously, there is the whole interaction of public opinion and media. We talk about islamophobic media in Europe, we talk about the way the media portray events in the Middle East and so on through a very particular prism, but it works the other way as well. Middle Eastern media have a peculiar view of what Europe and the West are like. I remember coming across a report in *al-Sharq al-Awsat*, the Saudi Arabian newspaper, about twenty years ago reporting that in one of the southern British towns on the coast, a redundant church had been sold to the local Muslim community to become a mosque. It had been done in full cooperation between the church and the Muslim community, it was the church community that had engaged in a serious constructive dialogue with the Muslims and were handing over this church to the Muslims as part of what they saw as their service of helping the Muslims to find a place and be at home. That was reported in *al-Sharq al-Awsat* as another Muslim conquest! However much we can be furious at the media for the distortion of news, for the selection of news, we cannot ignore it as it has an enormous impact on public opinion. As anyone who works in this kind of area in this country must know, it is frustrating and it is an uphill struggle, but it works the other way as well. It is like that everywhere.

In Europe the nation and the state and its borders have grown organically, have grown together out of a history. In a way the nation state ideology came in as a final confirmation and ideological confirmation of what have already come into existence in practise. But in the Middle East states were created within which nations had to be built with ensuing instability and uncertainty. If we turn this back on ourselves, and I think that is an important part of the dialogue we are not only talking about the Middle East and exporting democracy etc., we are actually experiencing ourselves some of what is going on in the Middle East. In the settlement after the Second World War we thought in Europe that we had got to the end of the process of the construction of nations, with all the bloodiness that comes about through wars of religion, then national wars, wars of irredentism etc. etc. from the 16th/17th century to the first half of the twentieth century. In Eastern Europe also, although with a different ideology, the nation had been made redundant through the solidarity of the working classes. But post-Soviet we are discovering that we have not sorted it out, so the issue of what it means to be British, Danish, German, French has been reopened. Hopefully not in such a bloody manner as the nation identifying process of the Balkans has been.

With immigration and settlement of new communities in Europe you can no longer talk about a white Lutheran Denmark. When I was in secondary school here in the early 1960s I had a classmate who was a Baptist. He was much more Danish than I was, but there were always questions raised about how one can be Danish and Baptist. The Muslim immigrants have saved my ex-classmate's Danishness, now the question is targeted at them. I suspect that the violence of the debate in Denmark actually relates to the fact that all of the various issues that are related to this have suddenly come together into the public sphere after 9/11 – can Muslims be Danish? We had that debate in Britain in 1989/90. Interestingly at that time the question was raised: can we trust these Muslims? Yes, they are British citizens but are they actually going to be *loyal* British citizens? At a time when we were invading, well at that time, in 1991, we were *liberating* Kuwait, there was not a single case recorded of a British Muslim in any way getting involved on the other side, i.e. fighting with the Iraqis. Still the question was not raised about Tony Benn or Edward Heath who was always against the war, we had the debate and we got over it.

It is very interesting that since 9/11 and the 2003 war that while we have actually had recorded cases of British Muslims fighting on the other side, the question about the general loyalty of the British Muslim community to the British state has not been raised. That debate was sorted out ten years ago. In Denmark everything has come together into one peaked clash. But I have my hopes that it is a small country with a very strong democratic tradition, much stronger than we have in Britain and that therefore you will solve your problems before we solve ours.

## What to do?

I think that one of the most important things that European countries and societies can do is to leave as much breathing space as possible for Muslims and other immigrant groups, whether they define themselves as Muslims or something else in this sense is beside the point. They should be given space to work out for themselves how to integrate functionally within their new society. The vast majorities want to and in my experience find very constructive ways of doing so without assimilating. Your Hassan does not become a Jørgen. He remains Hassan, but he becomes a Danish Hassan as distinct from a Kashmiri Hassan. If you give the breathing space, if you make a wide as possible public space available, the end result is going to be much more sustainable and healthy, whereas the moment government policies come in there is an element of restriction. There is of course here a border line which always has to be negotiated, but the more you restrict the options the more pathological the response will be.

I think one of the advantages of Britain is that there is much more space. Britain is by its founding mythology multinational. Englishness is explicitly multinational, a marriage between Anglo-Saxons and Normans. Since the Reformation Britain has been a multi-religious country to an extent that is not seen anywhere else in Europe, with a partial exception of the Netherlands. Thus it is much easier in a place like Britain to find a niche, a bit of space between some of the tectonic plates to fit in another community.

Historically in Britain the Catholics were for a long time regarded with much greater suspicion, considered a much greater danger than even the worst the anti-Islamic propaganda of the British National Party today talks about. There is a kind of accumulating experience there, and in some ways Denmark and France are at the opposite ends of the scale, Denmark with its very monolithic national tradition and national identity and France with its ideological *laïcisme republicain*. In those circumstances it is much more difficult to find space, to make space.

We are talking about an issue which will take two generations if not three to sort itself out. For a start we have fourteen hundred years of history behind us, much of it mythologised, and to change that is like changing the direction of a super tanker. It will need a nudge sideways and sideways; you cannot stop it head on. The most important response to my mind, taking the long term view, is education. It is the young people in school today and tomorrow and the day after tomorrow who are going to make the difference to public opinion, a generation down the line, which through the democratic processes and through the market processes of the media etc. will change the discourse. Education is absolutely central. One of the reasons why the situation in Britain is not rosy – and it is not – but on balance it is better than the rest of Europe – is because we have had over thirty years of multifaith religious education in schools. We have a whole generation of kids who have come out of school and, however bad the religious education has been, however bad and simplistic the education for example about Islam has been, there is some basic knowledge there so the politicians cannot get away with total misrepresentations, and the newspapers after all have to sell and they cannot carry on selling misrepresentations to an audience that does not buy it. Even *The Sun* a few weeks after 9/11 had a front page lead saying that al Qa'ida is not the same as our Muslims. Our Muslims are different. Followed a week later by an eight-page inside feature supplement looking at what is going on within the Muslim community and leaving Muslims, young and old, and community leaders, to speak for themselves. Part of the reason why they do that is because their market, the audience out there, has a minimum of knowledge about the basics of Islam and Muslims. Thus education is absolutely essential for a long term change.

# Biographies

**Abu-Khalid, Fowziyah** A poet and a professor of sociology at King Saud University, Riyadh, Saudi Arabia. Dr. Abu-Khalid is a graduate of Portland, Oregon, USA. She is a pioneer of writing free verse poetry in Saudi Arabia. She is also a pioneer of demanding a series of social and political reforms in Saudi Arabia, especially those related to the position and rights of Saudi women of full citizenship. One of her main contributions in this area was the Saudi government's response to the request of issuing an identity card for the Saudi women. A right that was historically denied.

**Aita, Samir** General Manager of A Concept Mafhoum. Ancien Elève de l'Ecole Polytéchnique, diplomed from the Ecole des Hautes Etudes en Sciences Sociales. He has spend 20 years working in the industry, before founding A Concept Mafhoum, a consulting and web editing firm.

**Al-Nu'aimi, Huda** Lecturer at the Iraqi Al-Mustansariyah University, Department of Political Science, Baghdad.

**Fergany, Nader** Director of Almishkat Centre for Research in Egypt. He is also Lead Author for the Arab Human Development Reports of 2002, 2003 and 2004. He obtained his Doctorate from the University of North Carolina, USA. He has taught and undertaken research at numerous institutions in Egypt and elsewhere and acted as a consultant to many Arab and international organisations. He has also published on demography, international migration, labour markets, education and development in the Arab world.

**Hinnebusch, Raymond** Professor of International Relations and Middle East Politics at the University of St. Andrews in Scotland. He is the author of *The International Relations of the Middle East*, Manchester University Press, 2003; *The Foreign Policies of Middle East States*, edited with A. Ehteshami, Boulder, CO, Lynne Rienner Press, 2001; *Syria, Revolution from Above*, Routledge, 2000; *Syria and the Middle East Peace Process*, with Alasdair Drysdale, Council on Foreign Relations Press, 1991, *Egyptian Politics under Sadat*, Cambridge, 1985.

**Nielsen, Jørgen S.** Educated in Arabic language and Middle Eastern studies in London and PhD in Arab history from the American University in Beirut, Lebanon. Since 1978 lecturer and later on professor in Islamic studies, first at Selly Oak College, Birmingham, and later at the University of Birmingham, where his research has mainly focused on Islam in Europe. Author of *Muslims in Western Europe*, 3rd ed., Edinburgh University Press, 2004, and co-author of *Muslims in the enlarged Europe: Religion and society*, Brill, 2003. From October 2005 Director of The Danish Institute in Damascus.

**Rabbani, Hanan Abdel Rahamn** Palestinian human rights/women's rights activist and development practitioner. She holds an MA from the Institute of Social Studies in The Hague, 1994. Worked for Al Haq, a prominent Palestinian human rights organisation 1988-1990. From 1997 to1999 she worked on a project entitled: "Palestinian Model Parliament on Women and Legislation". She has also worked for international organisations such as; Canadian International Development Agency (CIDA) in their Palestinian territories programme, and in Associates in Rural Development (ARD), an American consulting firm on a project entitled: "Strengthening the Capacity of the Palestinian Legislative Council". In Jordan where she is currently stationed, she worked as a consultant on Iraq for a number of International NGOs including Friedrich Naumann Foundation and Amnesty International. Currently she works with the Human Rights Office of the United Nations Assistance Mission for Iraq (UNAMI).

**Rahbek, Birgitte** PhD in cultural sociology and education. Author of *Arabiske kvindekår* (The Situation for Arab Women), *Børn mellem 2 kulturer* (Children Between Two Cultures), *Tro og skæbne i Jerusalem; virkeligheden* *bag Selma Lagerlöfs roman "Jerusalem"* (Belief and Faith in Jerusalem; the Reality Behind Selma Lagerlöf's novel "Jerusalem") together with Mogens Bähncke. *En stat for enhver pris* (A State at Any Price), 2000.

**Sayigh, Yezid** holds a Chair in Middle East Studies at King's College London. A former Palestinian advisor and negotiator, he is also the principal author (with Khalil Shikaki) of the Report of the Independent Task Force on Strengthening Palestinian Public Institutions (New York, Council on Foreign Relations, 1999). His publications include *Armed Struggle and the Search for a State: The Palestinian National Movement, 1949-1993*, Oxford University Press, 1997. He was a Visiting Professor at AUB (American University of Beirut) 2003-2004, and again 2005-2006. His academic research now focuses on the military and the state in the Middle East; on the relationship between religion and nationalism (especially Islam and Arab nationalisms) in the context of economic globalisation; and on political systems, institution-building, and political economies in transitional and post-conflict societies.

**Shlash, Amal Raouf** Born in Baghdad, Msc Economics, PhD Economics from the University of Salford, U.K 1983. Prof. of Economics of Development, University of Baghdad, major areas of teaching and research are development, and International Relations. Currently; President of Bayt al-Hikma in Baghdad, a think-tank and research-centre.

**Usher, Graham** Author and journalist, Palestine correspondent for MEI (Middle East International) and al Ahram English Weekly. He has been based in Jerusalem for many years. Author of *Palestine in Crises: The Struggle for Peace in Political Independence After Oslo*, Pluto Press, 1995; *Dispatches From Palestine: The Rise and Fall of the Oslo Peace Process*, Pluto Press, 1999.

**Yamani, Mai** Born a Saudi national and became one of the leading British experts on Saudi politics and society. Awarded a BA from Bryn Mawr College, Pennsylvania, and a doctorate from Oxford University in social anthropology, she lectured for three years at King Abdul Aziz University in Jeddah. For ten years she was academic adviser to the Centre for Contemporary Arab studies at Georgetown University, Washington DC. At the same time she served as Fellow at the Centre of Islamic and Middle

Eastern law at London University. She is now a research fellow with the Middle East Programme at the Royal Institute of International Affairs, Chatham House and writes and broadcasts frequently on Saudi affairs. Her publications include *"Changed Identities"* – *the challenge of the New Generation in Saudi Arabia,* 2000, and *The Rule of Law in the Middle East and the Islamic World,* co-editor, 2000; *Cradle of Islam* – *the Hijaz and the Quest for an Arabian Identity,* 2004.